W9-AMR-705

ST. VINCENT AND THE GRENADINES

BEQUIA, MUSTIQUE, CANOUAN, MAYREAU, TOBAGO CAYS, PALM, UNION, PSV

A PLURAL COUNTRY

Photographer
DANA JINKINS
Author
JILL BOBROW

With special contributions by Margaret Atwood,
Graeme Gibson, and Raquel Welch

Concepts Publishing

ST. VINCENT AND THE GRENADINES

EQUIA, MUSTIQUE, CANOUAN, MAYREAU, TOBAGO CAYS, PALM, UNION, PSV

PLURAL COUNTRY

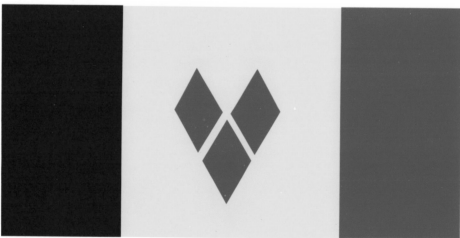

St. Vincent and the Grenadines; A Plural Country. Text copyright © 1985 by Dana Jinkins and Jill Bobrow. All rights reserved. Printed in Tokyo, Japan. No part of this book may be used or reproduced in any manner whatsoever without written permission except in the case of brief quotations embodied in critical articles and reviews. For information address W.W. Norton and Company, Inc. 500 Fifth Ave., New York, N.Y. 10110 or in the Caribbean address Tipi Punnett, P.O. Box 17, St. Vincent, West Indies.

Library of Congress Catalogue Card Number: 85–19470

ACKNOWLEDGEMENTS

Photographer/Designer:
DANA JINKINS

Author/Editor:
JILL BOBROW

Associate editor:
PAT MITCHELL

Contributing Writers:
MARGARET ATWOOD
GRAEME GIBSON
SHAKE KEANE

Art Director:
ELIZABETH PRINZ

Copyeditor:
JEREMY TOWNSEND

Illustrator:
RANDI JINKINS

Published by:
CONCEPTS PUBLISHING
P.O. Box 323
Warren, Vermont 05674

Distributed in the USA and Canada by:
W. W. NORTON & COMPANY INC.
500 Fifth Avenue
New York, New York 10110

Distributed in the Caribbean by:
TIPI PUNNETT
P.O. Box 17
St. Vincent, West Indies

Printed by:
DAI NIPPON PRINTING COMPANY
Tokyo, Japan

Many people assisted with the publication of this book. We would like to thank especially Dr. Earl Kirby, the Honorable Marcus DeFreitas, Dr. Kenneth John, Ken Boyea, Dr. Vivian Child, Michael Findlay, photographer P. Mickles, the New York design office of Jonson, Pedersen, Hinrichs, and Shakery, and the H.M.S. Arrow.

Photographs not taken by Dana Jinkins are individually accredited.

*I*t was Son Mitchell's idea for this book and, as a native of one of the smaller islands, the present Prime Minister of St. Vincent and the Grenadines knows as well as anyone the essential plurality of the country. He has told me that as a youth at school on the mainland of St. Vincent he did not hear for three days of his grandmother's death on the island of Bequia, nine miles distant. In those days it was sail alone—no motors, no telephones, no radios. If the wind did not blow, or, as sometimes happened, blew too much, the islands were totally disconnected. Fortunately, communications have improved. But insularity—of the islands within the country, and of the country vis-à-vis the outside world—is still the primary fact of life in this sovereign state.

There are challenges here certainly, but compensations too, in the stunning variety of landscape within the archipelago—the mist hanging over the hulk of the Soufrière, the tandem curves of cultivated terraces, brilliant flowers glowing against the characteristic lime-green of tropical vegetation, wind and sun-beaten stretches of coral sand, the omnipresent sea with its changeability, its authority. And above all the blessed clarity that unpolluted air alone can provide.

The photographs in this book encompass these pleasures and more. Some of the best, surely, are of the people, their natural gaiety and stoic grace, often in the face of difficult conditions. Anyone interested in discovering the spirit of St. Vincent and the Grenadines will be charmed by, and grateful to, the people here portrayed.

Jill Bobrow, who compiled the text, and Dana Jinkins, the photographer and designer, have been coming to these islands for many years. They have been responsible for most of this material either originally or in its selection, and the processing of it into book form. Special thanks are due to Margaret Atwood and Shake Keane for allowing us to include poems and to Margaret Atwood and Graeme Gibson, longtime visitors to the country, for the impressions composed especially for this publication.

Our gratitude also to Raquel Welch and Mary Wells Lawrence for providing an insight into their feelings for the islands.

Inevitably there are aspects of this very small but diverse nation not represented in these hundred-odd pages. But there is no doubt that what we do have is a remarkable document of great beauty. I hope the people of St. Vincent and the Grenadines will be proud of it, and of their own unique multi-island state.

Pat Mitchell

IMPRESSIONS

MARGARET ATWOOD

Landcrab I

A lie, that we come from water.
The truth is we were born
from stones, dragons, the sea's
teeth, as you testify,
with your crust and jagged scissors.

Hermit, hard socket
for a timid eye,
you're a soft gut scuttling
sideways, a blue skull,
round bone on the prowl.
wolf of treeroots and gravelly holes,
a mouth on stilts,
the husk of a small demon.

Attack, voracious
eating, and flight:
it's a sound routine
for staying alive on edges.

Then there's the tide, and that dance
you do for the moon
on wet sand, claws raised
to fend off your mate,
your coupling a quick
dry clatter of rocks.
For mammals
with their lobes and tubers,
scruples and warm milk,
you've nothing but contempt.

Here you are, a frozen scowl
targeted in flashlight,
then gone: a piece of what
we are, not all,
my stunted child, my momentary
face in the mirror,
my tiny nightmare.

MARGARET ATWOOD

When I first went to Bequia in 1973 I didn't think I would ever write anything about it. I thought it would be a place where I would get away from writing. I was going to see two friends of mine from college, who for one reason or another had both ended up there. I hadn't seen them for twelve years, which seemed improbable. The fact that they were both living on Bequia seemed improbable. Even my trip seemed improbable.

This was the first time I had ever been to a tropical country. What did I expect? Probably I thought I would meet Joseph Conrad sitting in a beach bar. It's hard to remember. I do remember that stepping off the plane was like walking into hot damp cotton wool, or magic: at night, on St. Vincent, the air was filled with the sound of small glass bells (made, it turned out, by a kind of "tree toad"), and the shoreline, palms with moon, looked disconcertingly like a postcard.

The next day there was the sail from St. Vincent to Bequia on the *Friendship Rose*, a creaking, motorized sailing ship I thought of as a schooner. This time it was Robert Louis Stevenson I expected to see. The heat of the sun seemed overdone, and made me feel albino.

As I sat under a palm tree that night, a skull walked out of a hole in the ground. I was not surprised to see it. Possibly I had sunstroke, and was hallucinating; on the other hand, nothing about this experience was, as yet, altogether believable, so a walking skull was not out of place.

Then I never would have thought that such events would acquire a kind of dailyness, that the Kodachrome gloss on the landscape would rub off, that I would reach a point at which I could absorb them, even take them for granted. The skull was only a landcrab after all, and common as coconuts, and edible.

But I began to understand why my two friends, once they'd reached Bequia, had never left.

This island was not a tourist trap, which was one of the reasons I liked it. You had to work a little to get there. There were ropes to be learned, ways of doing or not doing a thing. Only the sunsets were obvious; the beaches merely looked deserted. The people really lived there and had things to do. Also, they were curious: they wanted to know what you were up to, like any neighbor.

No one knows what causes an outer landscape to become an inner one, particularly for a writer. But after many visits to Bequia over a period of seven or eight years, I did at last begin to write about it.

The first poem was about the walking skull, my original and surreal encounter. After that, the poems moved back into particular history, out into unique space. They created for me an entrance into Bequia; perhaps my first genuine entrance, because writers are fated to be writers and there are no vacations, and how do you know you're really in a place until you've engaged it, asked it questions, found out at least some of its words?

Sometimes, finding a pattern in memory is like trying to untangle an impossible mess of fishing line—the more you persist, the more intractable knots and tangles become until, if time is short, all you can do is cut them out.

Islands are fascinating because of their separate cultures and histories, also the fulfillment they have found in relative isolation. Because of well defined limits each is, in some way, unique and often idiosyncratic.

Which brings me to the special relationship between islands and birds. Think of Darwin and his finches! Less isolated, and more thoroughly settled, Saint Vincent is clearly not so dramatic as the Galapagos, but its wonderful parrot, and the Whistling Warbler, are both endemic species. What is more, the Hooded Tanager is found only here and in Grenada. And others, the curiously endearing Trembler, three species of Hummingbird, and a bullfinch, are localized in the Lesser Antilles.

Since I love them it isn't surprising that some of my typical memories include the birds. Moreover it has usually been Earl Kirby who helped me.

Professionally a veterinarian, Dr. Kirby is a man with an infectious, and omnivorous curiosity about his country and its inhabitants. Himself a natural resource, Kirby's generous knowledge about the history, archaeology, the flora and fauna of Saint Vincent, makes him a memorable guide.

Sweating and stumbling, perhaps we follow as Kirby leads us beside a trickle of water in a rocky stream bed rising into the hills. It is 1973 and we hope to find the Saint Vincent Parrot.

Approaching the crest of a hill we hear parrots, a small gang of raucous voices high on a neighbouring ridge. It is a wonderful sound. But then, quite unexpectedly, we are engulfed in a tropical shower, a torrent that fills the stream bed in minutes, and soaks us entirely. The forest seems full of water and then, somewhere above us, the sun returns.

We don't see the parrots, not this trip, but on descending we encounter something as good—the rare and charming Whistling Warbler. Formal in black and white, it has an eye-ring that gives it a vaguely astonished look...

Or we are climbing Soufrière, on the windward side, before its last eruption. Beneath all this vegetation the land is hard. We walk on frozen rivers of rock, old rivers of fire.

Accustomed, as we are, to the relative simplicity of northern forests, this fecundity, the richness of growth and shade, is wonderfully strange. We've seen Hooded Tanagers, the Lesser Antillean Bullfinch, doves and a Purple-throated Carib Hummingbird. If we weren't in a hurry to reach the crater, if only there was more time, the day would be perfect.

Lagging behind, reluctant to pass out of the forest onto the bare hill, I see a Trembler, that lean, nervous bird; it is in a clearing among the foliage. And just as the book promised, its trembling! I'm enchanted. I'm enchanted by its name, by the delight of its odd behaviour, and the excitement, too, of seeing a bird that intrigued me so in the field guide...

Over on Bequia, if you go north to the end of the road, past Spring and Park, where the land is lower, wetter, with more flowering shrubs and trees, more palms, you will find the path to Shark Bay.

We have been there often, although never with Earl Kirby. It is a good walk, often hot, and each time we scramble over the last piles of stone, where a hill rises sharply to Brute Point, we're as delighted, as moved as we were on our first visit. Dramatic and very beautiful, Shark Bay lies, rocky and tumultuous, between two high, eroded points. Indeed it is almost completely surrounded by cliffs of black volcanic rock and the sea seems angry; it bursts and churns.

Often there are iguanas and once, peering over a precipice, we saw the cool shape of an enormous sea turtle basking in turquoise water. There are streamlined Tropicbirds, too, incredibly white against the rocks; there are nesting Boobies, Frigatebirds and a good variety of terns. Startled by our appearance, birds lift into the air but they don't go far; they wheel and drift above our heads...

We all have our own pre-occupations, our own compulsions. And of course there is more to this country, to these islands, than any of us will finally know.

MARGARET ATWOOD, GRAEME GIBSON AND THEIR DAUGHTER JESS.

GRAEME GIBSON IS A CANADIAN WRITER WHOSE NOVELS INCLUDE "PERPETUAL MOTION," "COMMUNION," AND "FIVE LEGS."

MARGARET ATWOOD IS RECOGNIZED AS ONE OF CANADA'S FOREMOST WRITERS. HER WORKS HAVE BEEN PUBLISHED IN FIFTEEN COUNTRIES AND IN TEN LANGUAGES. SHE AND GRAEME GIBSON AND THEIR DAUGHTER JESS HAVE VISITED ST. VINCENT AND THE GRENADINES MANY TIMES.

MARGARET ATWOOD IS A NOVELIST WHO HAS AUTHORED THE BOOKS "LIFE BEFORE MAN," "SURFACING," "BODILY HARM," AND MOST RECENTLY "THE HANDMAID'S TALE."

TABLE OF CONTENTS

HISTORY

1

S t. Vincent was discovered and settled long before Columbus landed there. Archeologists contend that life existed in the West Indies before the time of Christ. Indirect evidence points to St. Vincent being inhabited by a race called Siboney (or Ciboney) around the year 5000 B.C., who emigrated to the islands from South America. Among those moving north were the Arawak Indians. The Arawaks were believed to have been the largest prehistoric nation in South America. They had a peaceful agrarian civilization and called themselves "Lokono," meaning human beings.

They were tormented by another group of Indians whom they called Caribs (Charibs, Caraibes), meaning rebellious. The Caribs finally conquered the Arawaks, killing all the men but sparing the women. The combination of Arawak women and Carib men produced a strong race. The Caribs occupied Martinique, Dominica, St. Lucia, St. Vincent, and the Grenadines. They were the sole masters of these islands until the advent of the Europeans in the late fifteenth and early sixteenth centuries.

The land has its legends. One is that it was called Hairoun or "Land of the Blessed" by some Caribs. Another that it was Youroumei, which defined the serene beauty of the rainbows in the valleys. Yet it was the Spaniards who apparently had the strongest influence and named the island after their patron Saint; Saint Vincent.

Along with European settlers came their slaves—Negroes imported from Africa. Some of the first Negroes filtered into St. Vincent from Spanish ships that were wrecked off the coast of St. Vincent enroute to Santo Domingo. In 1675, a Dutch ship foundered off the east coast of Bequia. The Negroes were the only survivors. They were harbored by the Caribs on Bequia and subsequently came to St. Vincent where they were assimilated into the "Yellow," Carib i.e., pure Carib community.

Slaves from Barbados and from St. Lucia, hearing about St. Vincent as a colonial haven, also managed to escape to the island. By 1700 Negroes were well ensconced on St. Vincent. The mixture of the Negro Caribs resulted in a new group called the "Black Caribs." As the Black Caribs increased in number and grew stronger, the Yellow Caribs felt threatened and asked assistance from the governor of Martinique.

In 1700 St. Vincent was divided. The west went to the Yellow Caribs and the east to the Black Caribs. The French initially were allies of the Yellow Caribs. In the early 1700s they attempted to defeat the Black Caribs but were unsuccessful. The French then decided to live in harmony with both Yellow and Black Caribs. The French considered St. Vincent their home and were content to grow indigo, cotton, tobacco, and a small amount of sugar with the help of their own slaves. Because it was difficult to distinguish these slaves

1-2. *CAPTAIN BLIGH PICTURE* ORIGINALLY COMMISSIONED AS A COMMEMORATIVE CHRISTMAS CARD FOR THE ROYAL SOCIETY IN BRITAIN THIS PAINTING BY THE WELL-KNOWN BRITISH PROTRAITIST ANNA ZINKEISON, DEPICTS THE ILLUSTRIOUS CAPTAIN BLIGH ARRIVING IN ST. VINCENT WITH THE FIRST BREADFRUIT TREE, A SLIP OF WHICH STILL FLOURISHES IN KINGSTOWN'S BOTANIC GARDENS.

2

from many of the Black Caribs, the latter adopted the custom of flattening the skulls of their babies between two boards which they tightened progressively at both ends. The resulting sloped forehead is exhibited in some of the artifacts that have been discovered in St. Vincent.

The Black Caribs adopted customs from both the Yellow Caribs and the French. The French, seeking to be on compatible terms with the Black Caribs, sent missionaries to live among them and The Black Caribs adopted many French names such as Pierre Gateau, Chatoyer, and Jean Baptiste. They also established small farms similar to the French farms. There is a place in St. Vincent today known as Duvallé which was the site of a Black Carib cotton plantation.

While the French eased into St. Vincent, the English came officiously, justifying their presence with a series of royal grants and treaties starting in 1627. The first significant attempt at colonization came in 1722 when George I gave St. Vincent and St. Lucia to the Duke of Montague. A Captain Braithwaite was sent to St. Vincent to form a settlement. It was only after the Treaty of Paris in 1763 that St. Vincent was ceded to the English, and settlers began inundating the island.

The best area for the growth of sugar was the Carib country called Grand Sable which stretched from Byera River to Rabacca. Despite opposition from the French and the Black Caribs, the English continued to appropriate lands. The British also tried to impose their laws on the Caribs in the form of a peace treaty in 1773. Although the treaty was signed by several Black Caribs, including Chief Chatoyer, it is inconceivable that the Caribs (who communicated in the French language) understood the implications of the restrictions enumerated in the English treaty.

In 1779, the Black Caribs once again enlisted the help of the French from Martinique in an attempt to oust the English. In 1782, however, the Treaty of Versailles insured that the French would depart St. Vincent and leave the Black Caribs to their own devices. Soon the ideas inspired by the French Revolution reached the Caribbean. After a successful uprising in Guadeloupe, a French radical, Victor Hughes, incited Chief Chatoyer from the Leeward side and Duvallé from the Windward side to join forces with their French allies and converge on Kingstown to attack the English. The English suspected the planned attack and were on guard. The result was known as the second Carib War. Duvallé rampaged across the north Windward side burning the sugar works and killing as many Englishmen as he could. After his exploits he took over Dorsetshire Hill, pulled down the British flag, and raised the flag of the French Republic. Chief Chatoyer, coming from Chateaubelair, killed many English settlers but did not destroy their property. He

1

1. "A NEGRO FESTIVAL"—FROM AN ORIGINAL PICTURE BY AGOSTINO BRUNYAS—ORIGINALLY PUBLISHED NOV. 18, 1794 BY I. STOCKDALE, PICADILLY
2. "CHATOYER THE CHIEF OF THE BLACK CHARAIBES IN ST. VINCENT WITH HIS FIVE WIVES" FROM AN ORIGINAL PAINTING BY AGOSTINO BRUNYAS IN 1773.

then joined Duvallé at Dorsetshire Hill. Chatoyer, by all historical accounts, was an intelligent charismatic leader. His followers considered him invincible. Legend has it that Chatoyer's hubris led him to challenge British Major Leith to a duel. The latter, who was most proficient at swords, killed the chief. Chatoyer's followers were not as effective after his death. Today, Major Leith's remains are buried under the chandelier of the Anglican Cathedral in Kingstown and there is an obelisk honoring Chatoyer at Dorsetshire Hill.

In 1796 General Abercromby, dispatched from England to put down the Caribs, first overtook St. Lucia. Without the support of the French on St. Lucia, the Black Caribs were overpowered, and eventually surrendered to the English. The English settlers, embittered and fearful of the Caribs, recommended that they be banished from St. Vincent. A plan was executed to send the Caribs to Roatan in the Bay Islands of Honduras. Initially about 280 Caribs went to Balliceaux enroute to Roatan. Many Caribs still in St. Vincent, disappeared and hid from the English troops while others continued to ambush their oppressors. General Abercromby proved a formidable force and saw to it that Grand Sable was destroyed by fire. By 1797 some 5,080 Caribs surrendered and were taken to Balliceaux and then shipped to Roatan.

Meanwhile, the Yellow Caribs who had not been involved in all of the hostilities were given some land at Old Sandy Bay, and eventually were relocated at New Sandy Bay. The few remaining Black Caribs who did not surrender drifted into the bush in the area now called Greiggs. Later they were given a reservation beneath Petit Bonhomme. Some Caribs on the Leeward side stuck it out at the Morne Ronde area but fled prior to the 1812 eruption of the

1

2   3

volcano. That year a few more migrated to Trinidad. When one speaks of the Carib Indians today they are generally referring to the few descendants of the Yellow Caribs at Sandy Bay.

The history of St. Vincent is different from the other islands which were occupied by French, British, Spanish, and Dutch settlers. The Caribs put up such fierce opposition to the English settlers that for years the island was in a perpetual state of war. Consequently, St. Vincent never fully shared in the eighteenth century boom of the sugar islands.

Eight years after the emancipation of the slaves in 1838, Portuguese were introduced from Madeira who quickly collared the shopkeeping and small trading business. There followed in 1861 the start of an organised scheme of importation of Indian indentured servants to replace the Africans who fled the dehumanising conditions of the plantation. English immigrants who had sought refuge in Barbados from Cromwellian Britain later came over to St. Vincent and settled in Dorsetshire Hill, or moved to Mt. Pleasant in Bequia.

A cosmopolitan population thus grew out of the matrix of a pluralistic society. During the recent past, however, the island has been markedly free of the semblance of racial conflict or colour-based social tension owing, perhaps, to the pervasiveness of the Christian ethic and the dominance of the democratic ethos.

1. "WHEN SHALL WE THREE MEET AGAIN", ST. VINCENT, 1907
2. ROZEAU DRY RIVER—BOILING MUD—ST. VINCENT, 1902
3. "SOUFRIÈRE—WINDWARD ASCENT ABOVE LOT 14", ST. VINCENT, JUNE, 1902
4. FROM L. W.N. SANDS, DUNCAN MACDONALD & T.A. MACDONALD WITH TWO SERVANT GIRLS. (AT WALLILABOU, ST. VINCENT) 1907

4

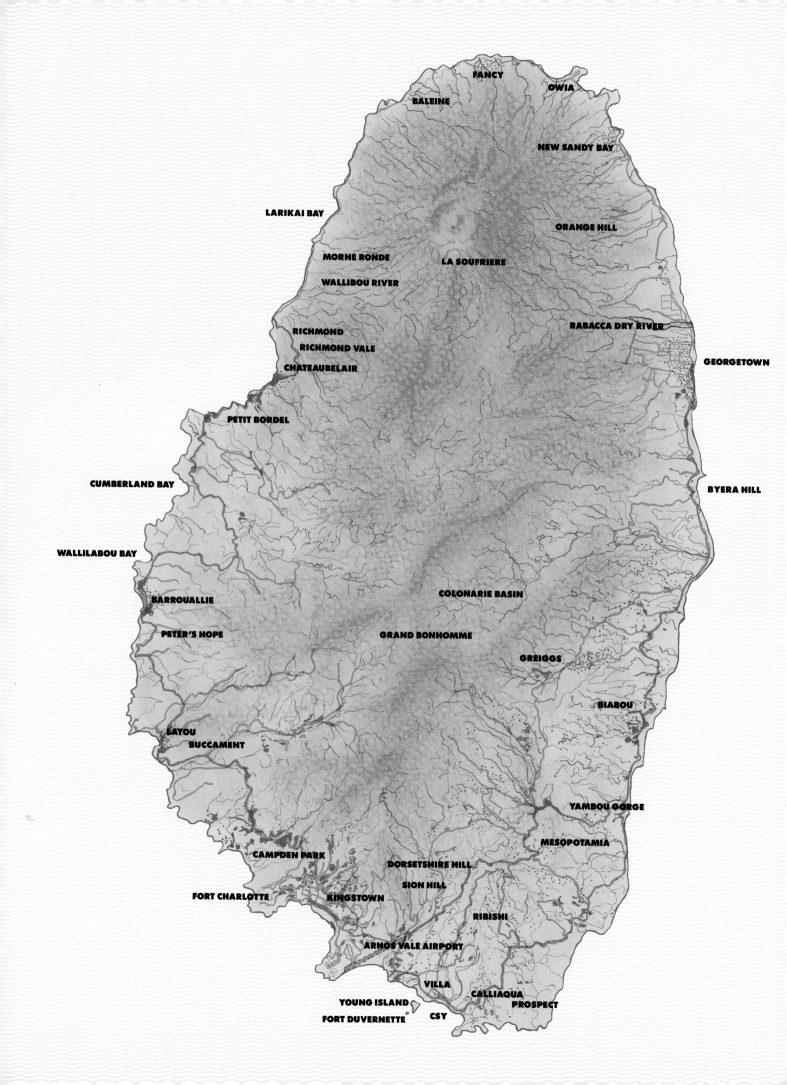

ST. VINCENT

St. Vincent and the Grenadines constitute an independent nation in the Windward Islands at the southern end of the Caribbean chain. St. Vincent lies on the latitude 13° 15' north and the longitude 60° 56' west. A densely green and mountainous island, it measures 18½ miles long and 11¼ miles wide, covering 345 square kilometers. The population is about 110,000. The capital is Kingstown and its population is about 23,000. The Grenadines are a chain of 32 odd islands, rocks and islets between St. Vincent to the north, and Grenada to the south. In combination with the St. Vincent owned Grenadines, the total territory covers 389 square kilometers, or 150 square miles. St. Vincent is approximately 1770 nautical miles from New York and about 90 miles west of Barbados.

St. Vincent is a verdant fertile country, cultivated by hardworking farmers. These farmers have made the country into the garden of the Caribbean.

History has left its mark in the names of towns and villages. The Spaniards who enjoyed a nodding acquaintance with the island left 'Point Espagnol'. The French who disputed the British claim left their imprint on other areas like Chateaubelair, Petit Bordel, Mustique and Sans Souci. Staid names like Kingstown, Georgetown and Argyle reflect the British tradition. The Caribs impressed names like Owia, Larakai, and one wonders how they sorted out hybrids with the French such as Tourama, Wallilabou, or with the Spaniards to produce Calliaqua.

Geology explains that the island rocked in its emergence from the sea, producing great depths beside its leeward coast and inland sea cliffs with shells and a second more recent coastline on the windward coast.

A "dollar bus" or a taxi are the best ways to get around the island. Close to town is the handicraft center where strawbaskets, jewelry, wall hangings, and other items may be obtained. Also just a walk from town are the Botanical Gardens and the Catholic, Anglican and Methodist Churches. If you drive up the Leeward coast, you can visit Fort Charlotte. Completed in 1806, the fort is on a ridge 600 feet above the sea in the former officers quarters, giving a fabulous view of Kingstown overlooking the Grenadines. There is a museum with paintings by Lindsay Prescott depicting Black Carib history of the island. Also at the fort is a bakery selling bread produced by prisoners for the hospitals, prisons, and other public institutions.

Further up the Leeward coast, is the Buccament Valley, with beautiful trails leading through tropical rain forests. Here is the chance to see or hear the St. Vincent Parrot and the whistling warbler, both unique to St. Vincent. This is also the habitat for the black hawk, the cocoa thrush, the crested hummingbird, the red-capped green tanager, green heron and a host of other interesting species. Also nearby are the Aquaduct Golf Course and the Casino. The golf course takes you through picturesque scenery with a breathtaking backdrop of high mountains and gentle streams.

Continuing on a tour up the Leeward coast are the towns of Layou, Barrouallie, Troumaca, Chateaubelair, and Richmond. Along the way you'll see the tobacco plantation Peter's Hope. North of Barrouallie is Wallilabou where there is a yacht anchorage and a batik workshop.

The most magnificent waterfall in St. Vincent is the Falls of Baleine. Accessible only by boat, it is seventeen and a half miles north of Richmond Beach on the northern end of the island. You can arrange with fishermen to ferry you to where the stream meets the sea and then it is an interesting short hike to the waterfall. The water comes from the volcanic hills and is sparkling and silky looking, and water pitches dramatically from about 100 feet to a swimming basin at the bottom. Not frequented by many tourists, this trip is quite an adventure. Another waterfall rarely visited is Trinity Falls up the Wallibou River.

Back in Kingstown and heading up the windward side you reach the airport of Arnos Vale. From there take Queens Drive to the high point of Dorsetshire Hill, and then come down Sion Hill to witness the sensational views over Kingstown, the harbor, and Fort Charlotte. Another worthwhile visit is the Harmony Hill Sugar Mill. From Kingstown, go through Calliaqua and then turn left on to the road to Ribishi. The windmill tower is still fairly complete

P. MICKLES

9

1

dating from the last quarter of the nineteenth century.

Further up the Windward side is Biabou, Sans Souci, Colonarie, and Georgetown. Up here are way stations for the Banana Growers Association, also the arrowroot plant at Mt. Bentinck and Mt. Bentinck rum distillery. Still further north is Orange Hill Estates and the mountain volcano, La Soufriére.

The most amazing drive on this side of the island is through the lush Mesopotamia Valley. This area is planted with bananas, tannias and dasheen. Mountain ridges rise all around. Bonhomme at 3,181 feet dominates the landscape. Streams and rivers come together at Mesopotamia to tumble down to the sea or over the rocks of the Yambou Gorge.

Montreal Gardens in the Mesopotamia Valley, is like an Alice in Wonderland world, with beautiful well-cared for gardens featuring Anthurium lilies — that unusual flower that is a bit waxy and appears to be sticking its tongue out at you. In the gardens, is one little honeymoon cottage (sometimes rented out) perched above the proverbial babbling brook.

Further up the Windward side is Biabou, Sans Souci, Colonarie, and the Georgetown. Up here are way stations for the Banana Growers Association, also the arrowroot plant at Mt. Bentinck and Mt. Bentinck rum distillery. Still further north is Orange Hill Estates and the mountain volcano, La Soufrière.

The remote northern end of the island is mainly populated by Caribs in the villages of Sandy Bay, Owia, and Fancy.

If you are interested in a Caribbean vacation not only to lie on a beach all day, but also to explore, St. Vincent is the ideal place. The countryside is breathtakingly beautiful and landscaped with farms, and the people of the small villages are friendly.

2

1. VIEW OF KINGSTOWN FROM DORSETSHIRE HILL.
2. THE *FRIENDSHIP ROSE* ARRIVING AT THE GRENADINES DOCK IN KINGSTOWN.
3. CARGO BOATS AT THE TOWN DOCK.

3

1

DONALD DERIGGS

2

MARY BARNARD

1. A VICTORY PARADE FOLLOWING
THE GENERAL ELECTION WON BY THE
NEW DEMOCRATIC PARTY.
2. FORT CHARLOTTE.
3 THE PARLIAMENT BUILDING.

3

GOVERNMENT

The St. Vincent government system is based on the British Westminster style of government. There are 13 constituencies, in each of which one member is elected by adult suffrage. One of these becomes the Prime Minister who then appoints a cabinet from amongst the elected members.

There is a Governor General chosen by the Prime Minister as the Queen's representative, a mainly ceremonial position. St. Vincent is an independent country but part of the British Commonwealth. St. Vincent also is a member of Caricom, an economic organization of several Caribbean countries, and of the Organization of American States.

In the summer of 1984, the general election was won by the New Democratic Party. The popular leader Son Mitchell became Prime Minister.

President Reagan, sensitive to the elections that were soon to follow in neighboring Grenada and the United States' role in that country, sent congratulations to the new Prime Minister:

"The democratic governments of the Eastern Caribbean are inspiring examples to other countries in the Western Hemisphere. We are certain that the bonds forged between us will be further strengthened in the future as we work together to promote democratic values in the Caribbean Region."

JOHN MACGRUER

1

1. BAY STREET, KINGSTOWN.
2. STREET STALLS OFFER A WIDE VARIETY OF ITEMS.
3. JOY SPROTT IS PROUD OF HER ORIGINAL DESIGNS. FASHION IS IMPORTANT TO THE MODERN VINCENTIAN WOMAN.
4. THE MARKET IS USUALLY REPLETE WITH FRESH FRUIT AND VEGETABLES FROM ALL OVER THE COUNTRY.

2

*B*ay St. is the colorful waterfront center for shops and a few hotels. The two most popular hotels in Kingstown for the businessman and overnight guest are the Heron and the Cobblestone Inn. The Heron, with its courtyard veranda is a modest hotel, right out of a Somerset Maugham novel. The Cobblestone Inn is a beautiful old stone building with arches and ivy-covered walls. A shopping arcade through the hotel passageway connects Bay Street with Middle Street.

4

3

1

1. TWO YOUNG STREET VENDORS
EXHIBIT AN ENTREPRENEURIAL
SPIRIT.
2. FLORA GUNN OPENED THE FIRST
HEALTH FOOD STORE ON MIDDLE
STREET, KINGSTOWN. THE SHOP IS AN
EXTENSION OF HER HEALTH CLUB IN
VILLA.
3. BACK STREET, KINGSTOWN.
4. NO CARIBBEAN TOWN HAS MORE
STONE ARCHES AND COBBLESTONES
THAN KINGSTOWN.

2

3

4

DICK NEVERSON

1

1. THE RED ANGEL STAINED GLASS WINDOW IN THE ANGLICAN CHURCH.
2. THE METHODIST CHURCH.
3. THE ANGLICAN CHURCH IS IN THE FOREGROUND AND THE CATHOLIC CHURCH IS IN THE BACKGROUND.

2

KENNETH MITCHNICK

3

KENNETH MITCHNICK

CHURCHES

M ost Vincentians are religious. On Sunday mornings the people dress in their finest and attend services. The three dominant churches are Anglican, Catholic, and Methodist. St. George's Anglican Cathedral in Kingstown is an example of Georgian architecture, the nave and the lower stages of the tower date from around 1820. There are some beautiful stained glass windows, three on the east, by Kempe and one large one on the south, of Munich glass. The Red Angel window has quite a history. It was commissioned by Queen Victoria for St. Paul's Cathedral in memory of her first grandson, the Duke of Clarence and Avondale, the son of the then Prince of Wales who became King Edward VII. She rejected it because angels were described in the Bible as clad in white. It was in storage in St. Paul's for many years until Bishop Jackson on holiday in London, was given the window by Dean Inge and he brought it to St. Vincent to replace the old window that was there.

St. Mary's Roman Catholic Cathedral, school and presbytery was originally built in 1823, enlarged in 1877 and 1891 and then renovated in the early 1940s by the Belgian priest Dom Charles Verbeke. This is truly ecclesiastical eclectic architecture; there are Romanesque arches, Gothic spires, and delicate embellishments, somewhat Moorish in design. The balconies, battlements, turrets and courtyard were among the last things to be added.

The Methodist church is just across the road with its distinctive diamond-shaped latticed windows.

Many other faiths are in ascendancy including Seventh Day Adventists, Baptists, and other missions.

The Botanical Gardens, on the western side of Kingstown, occupy approximately twenty acres. Established in 1765, the Gardens are the oldest of their kind in the Western Hemisphere. They are said "to have been established for the propagation of plants useful in medicine and profitable as articles of trade commerce for the benefit of his Majesty's colonies." The first cloves came from Martinique in 1787 and the first nutmegs from Cayenne in 1809. The most famous acquisition was the breadfruit plant procured by the notorious Captian Bligh. Years after the Mutiny on the Bounty, Bligh made a trip aboard the H.M.S. Providence to the South Pacific. He obtained plants which he brought to St. Vincent January 23, 1793. Three hundred plants remained in St. Vincent, the rest were carried to Jamaica. Breadfruit was used as cheap food for the slaves.

The breadfruit tree grows to about fifty feet in height, has a well-shaped trunk, and many branches. The leaves are large and distinctive. Locals say that a tea can be made from the leaves that is an efficacious remedy for high

2

1

SON MITCHELL

3

PAT MITCHELL

5

4

1. FRANGIPANI.
2. HELICONIA.
3. JADE VINE.
4. BREADFRUIT WAS FIRST BROUGHT
TO ST. VINCENT FROM THE SOUTH
PACIFIC BY CAPTAIN BLIGH.
5. "POOR MAN'S ORCHID."
6. ANTHURIUM LILIES.

6

1

1. HIBISCUS.
2. YELLOW POUI.
3. THE PRIME MINISTER'S RESIDENCE
IS SEEN IN THE DISTANCE ABOVE THE
BOTANICAL GARDENS.
4. THE LILY POND IN THE BOTANICAL
GARDENS.

blood pressure. The fruit is large, bumpy and green to start with and yellow when ripe. It can be baked, boiled, or roasted and keeps a long time when cooked. There is also a gum derived from the breadfruit tree that can be used for caulking boats, and a coarse cloth can be made from the inner fiber of the bark. All in all, it was a worthy item for Bligh to have brought to St. Vincent.

Dr. George Young, a medical officer and an avid horticulturist, was the first curator of the Botanical Gardens. By 1773, the gardens had quite a reputation. In 1783, Dr. Alexander Anderson succeeded Young and contributed greatly to experimentation and propagation. It was Anderson who tended the plants that Captain Bligh brought. A specimen from one of the original plants of 1793 still stands. This specimen is distinguished from most of the other breadfruit plants on the island because of its deeply indented leaves.

A Frenchman from Martinique, General de Bouille, was also an influence on the gardens. Through his efforts, black pepper and nutmeg were received from the French Guiana. After Anderson's death, the gardens had a couple of ineffectual curators and then were relinquished to the care of the colonial government. The first half of the nineteenth century was not an auspicious time for the gardens. It wasn't until 1890 that the gardens were resuscitated. From then on, despite hurricanes and financial problems, the gardens have continued to thrive. In the early 1900s a tiny Doric temple with an allamanda fountain next to a lily pond was constructed, and roads and benches were provided.

Today the island's gardens provide a peaceful spot to walk and admire the many different kinds of trees and flowering plants. Among them you can see the red flamboyant, yellow poui, the varied species of hibiscuses, bougainvillea, ixora, frangipanis, jacarandas, and wild orchids. The list of trees goes on and on: mahogany, teak, red cedar, banyan, rubber and African tulip, among them. There are also numerous palms and hedges. In fact, every kind of fruit and flower that is to be found in the tropics is surely represented. It is the most ornate garden in the Caribbean.

2

SON MITCHELL

3

4

TROMSON MONROE

1

The national bird of St. Vincent is the St. Vincent Parrot (Amazona guildingii). A species unique to this island, it is a colorful creature about sixteen to eighteen inches long, with a white, yellow, and violet head. The neck is mostly green and the body plummage is a tawny brown-gold. The wings are variegated, and the tail is green, blue, and yellow-tipped. Because of illegal exporting of the St. Vincent Parrot, the bird is becoming more and more scarce.

1. THE VINCENTIAN PARROT HAS BECOME AN ENDANGERED SPECIES.
2. PETROGLYPHS.
3. THIS EFFIGY STAND, FOUND IN THE ARNOS VALE SWAMP IS A "MODIFIED SALADOID (BARRANCOID)," CIRCA 350-700 A.D. IT IS ONE OF THE MANY ARTIFACTS IN THE ST. VINCENT NATIONAL MUSEUM.
4. THIS ANDESITE HEAD FOUND IN THE SEA DURING A LAND RECLAMATION IS CIRCA 1500. IT SHOWS THE FLATTENED FOREHEAD OF THE CARIB.

*L*ocated in the Botanical Gardens, the St. Vincent National Museum has been open since 1979, and contains numerous petroglyphs and work stones left by Pre-Columbian Indians which have been found in St. Vincent and some of the other islands in the Grenadines. The best-known petroglyph is located in Layou on the Leeward side. It is a singular stone more than twenty-feet long situated on the right bank of the river with faces incised into the rock.

Stone carvings depicting rayed heads can be seen elsewhere in St. Vincent at Barrouallie and Yambou. Besides carvings, work stones (that is, stones with depressions in them) have been found in numerous places such as Chateaubelair, Petit Bordel, and Troumaca Bay. Earle Kirby has written an illustrated chronicle which lists and exemplifies all of his findings on Pre-Columbian monuments. He is also the curator and the driving force behind the museum. Some of his explorations have led to spectacular discoveries such as the head of a Negro with a flattened forehead done by the Caribs and the incredible effigy piece found at Arnos Vale swamp by one of his assistants.

2

3

4

1

SPORTS

St. Vincent and the Grenadines is a sports-loving country and Vincentians actively participate in several sports and games at various levels, some doing so with great success at the international level.

Cricket, the Caribbean's leading sport, is followed in the state with the same passion as Brazilians follow soccer, New Zealanders follow Rugby and Americans follow baseball. Four Vincentians have played for the West Indies at international level—Charlie Ollivierre, a fast bowler, was a member of the first West Indian team to tour England in 1906. Following the tour he was recruited to play for Derbyshire, thus, with Sir Pelham Warner, he became the first West Indian to be recruited for English Country Cricket Clubs.

Football, although the most popular game in the country in terms of its wider player-appeal, is not as prestigious as cricket is to West Indians. St. Vincent and the Grenadines were twice runners-up in the Caribbean football Union's regional championship.

Netball is the most popular sport for women on the island and St. Vincent and the Grenadines has won the Caribbean Netball Championship on five occasions. Squash is also a popular sport.

Dr. Cyrus's squash court beneath his clinic was the only one on the island from 1966 to 1978. Today there are a total of eight squash courts. The newest complex has three national championship squash courts built to International Squash Rackets Federation specifications. A series of Caribbean championships have been played in St. Vincent.

The fitness craze prevalent around the world is also popular in St. Vincent. Under the influence of Tracy Connell, Flora Gunn, and Cornel Ferris, several exercise and dance studios are cropping up. Also joggers can be seen along the roads and beaches.

Basketball, table tennis, volleyball and bodybuilding all have their fans. And, of course, there are the usual tourist activities of tennis, golf, swimming, diving, and sailing. The latter have been a way of life for islanders long before there were tourists but tennis in particular is rapidly spreading.

Windsurfing, a natural in the warm waters of the Caribbean, is increasingly popular among both visitors and local enthusiasts.

2

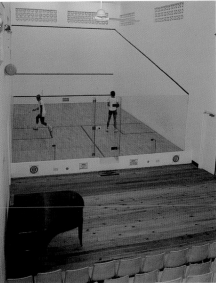

1. CRICKET IS THE MOST POPULAR
SPORT IN ST. VINCENT.
2. DANCE CLASSES ARE BECOMING
INCREASINGLY POPULAR AMONG THE
YOUNGER SET.
3. DR. CYRUS, LONG AN ENTHUSIAST
OF SQUASH HAS BUILT A SQUASH
COMPLEX.

3

1. BANANA TREES GROW WITH WHAT IS CALLED THE "MONKEY'S TAIL."
2. BANANAS ARE TRANSPORTED TO TOWN ON WEDNESDAYS AND LOADED ON THE GEEST BOAT.
3. PREPARING THE BANANAS FOR EXPORT.
4. A MAN IS LOADING ARROWROOT ON TO A CONVEYOR BELT TO BE WASHED AND PROCESSED.
5. BOXING TAKES PLACE IN THE FIELDS.

S t. Vincent's economy is dominated by the agricultural sector. The soil, of volcanic origin, is deep, well-drained, and extremely fertile. The annual rainfall ranges from sixty inches on the coastal areas to ninety to one hundred inches in the higher valleys. The rainfall is fairly well distributed throughout the year so that crop production is sustained year round.

Agriculture provides 65% of total employment. Bananas are the single most valuable export commodity. Approximately 6,200 acres of land are under production, the vast majority of which is on the Windward side of the island. There is increased interest on the Leeward side in bananas, particularly in the Richmond Vale area. At the end of 1983, there were 9,382 registered banana growers and 27,892 tons of bananas were exported in 1983. Bananas are either packed in the field or at boxing plants. Once a week the

3

4

5

Geest Boat comes to Kingstown Harbor to load and ship them to England.

Arrowroot is the second major export with about 1,000 acres under cultivation. Arrowroot was so named because it was used as an antidote to poisoned arrows. It is a tropical American plant of the genus Maranta with large leaves, white flowers and starchy rhizomes.

The harvesting season takes place between November and March. Rhizomes are laboriously dug out with hoes, transported to the factories, washed, ground, mixed in water, strained and allowed to settle in vast trays.

1. MANGOES ARE ONE OF ST. VINCENT'S MAJOR EXOTIC FRUIT EXPORTS.
2. PRIZE PUMPKINS AND OTHER VEGETABLES ARE LOADED ONTO A TRUCK.
3. GATHERING CABBAGES.
4. HILLSIDE CULTIVATION.

Arrowroot is the world's most digestible starch and is used as a thickener in cooking. It produces a translucent gravy. In the spice section of supermarkets you may see arrowroot from St. Vincent, one of the few countries in the world to make this unique product.

About 6,500 acres on the northeast and mideast coasts of St. Vincent are planted in coconuts, mainly used for the production of oil and soap.

The Department of Agriculture is currently very interested in encouraging all aspects of agriculture from backyard gardens to commercial enterprises. The Taiwanese are helping Vincentians with a hill rice crop as well as other vegetables such as asparagus. Other foreign organizations are also providing technical assistance. The most important aspect of present agricultural policy is the encouragement of the small independent farmer.

The market in Kingstown is replete with fruits and vegetables such as tannias, dasheen, sweet potatoes, carrots, eddoes, yams, pumpkins, pigeon peas, tomatoes, mangoes, citrus, pineapple, soursop, and sapodillas.

Other commercial crops include carrots, ginger, and recently tobacco. Crops such as ground provisions and peanuts fluctuate with price changes. Livestock is increasing, particularly cows, pigs, goats, and sheep. Another untapped potential market is for anthurium lilies, other cut flowers, and ornamentals.

JOHN MACGRUER

*T*he principal industrial estate is located at Campden Park about three miles west of Kingstown. The estate is approximately thirty acres and sustains various business enterprises. The Development Corporation constructs factory shells and rents space for enclave and other types of industry.

The largest operation at Campden Park is the East Caribbean Flour Mill. Conceived by P.H. Viera in 1966, the company was established as a joint venture operation. In 1977 with investment from government, private local and foreign concerns, the mill realized success. Working with Maple Leaf Mills Ltd. of Toronto, Canada, the E.C.F.M. produces and sells flour within the seven member territory of the East Caribbean Common Market.

Under the brand name "Cream of the Islands," 2400 (100lb) bags are produced per day. Both whole wheat and white flour are sold to all of the Caricom countries including St. Lucia, Dominica, Montserrat, and St. Kitts. With the by-product of the milling process animal feed is also produced. The flour mill employs about 150 people and the feed mill has 45 employees.

The entire operation is modern, clean, and efficient. Under the management of Ken Boyea, the workers seem to enjoy a feeling of camaraderie and to take pride in their work. Visitors from North America find it difficult to understand the high level of efficiency achieved in such a relaxed atmosphere. Boyea has established employee benefit programs which include training and management schemes and additional personal amenities such as playing fields for football (soccer) and cricket, and there is even a cooperative vegetable garden.

Elsewhere on the industrial compound is St. Vincent Sporting Goods which manufactures Wilson tennis rackets. Operations were started in St. Vincent January, 1983. The Pro Staff family, Wilson's top-of-the-line rackets,

2

1

3

1. CONTAINER SHIPS MAKE FREQUENT
STOPS IN ST. VINCENT.
2. BAGS OF FEED ARE SHIPPED TO
OTHER CARICOM COUNTRIES.
3. CAMPDEN INDUSTRIAL PARK IS
IN A STAGE OF GROWTH AND
DEVELOPMENT.
4. THE OFFICE AT THE EAST
CARIBBEAN FLOUR MILLS LTD.

4

1

2

made from graphite and kevlar, are being produced exclusively in St. Vincent. Wes Rutt and a handful of other Americans are training Vincentians for management. At present there are 160 Vincentians employed there.

St. Vincent Children's Wear which carries the Polly Flinders label is also manufactured at Campden Industrial Park. Hand smocking is done here, and over 200 dozen dresses are produced a day. There are 219 employees who work on an incentive plan. They are paid their daily wage plus a bonus for extra work accomplished.

Cardboard containers, and furniture are also manufactured in St. Vincent. There are a variety of small businesses involving garment making and the bottling of local products such as jams, herbs, and condiments. A special treat are St. Vincent peanuts, rated by many as the best tasting in the world. But it's the packaging that is quite ingenious; the peanuts are put in recycled beer bottles!

Manufacturing is new to this agrarian society. However, experienced industrialists are amazed how quickly Vincentian workers learn new technology. Productivity excels; perhaps it is the Protestant work ethic.

3

4

1. ST. VINCENT SPORTING GOODS
STARTED MANUFACTURING WILSON
PRO-STAFF FAMILY OF TENNIS
RACKETS IN 1983.
2. FURNITURE FABRICATION IS A
SMALL, BUT GROWING INDUSTRY.
3. THE TAIWANESE ARE TEACHING
VINCENTIANS TO MAKE LAMPS AND
BASKETS OUT OF BAMBOO.
4. THE SMOCKING FACTORY EMPLOYS
AROUND 220 PEOPLE.
5. A YOUNG WOMAN IS WORKING ON
THE INCENTIVE PLAN AT THE
SMOCKING PLANT.

5

1

2

4

3

5

1. MESOPOTAMIA VALLEY IS EVERY BIT AS LUSH AS ITS BIBLICAL NAMESAKE.
2. GINGERBREAD IS OFTEN A MOTIF ON OLDER VINCENTIAN HOMES.
3. SASHA AND ART AREN'T A BIT SHY.
4. A MODERN HOME, NEWLY BUILT IN RATHO MILL.
5. UNION PLANTATION.
6. DR. CECIL CYRUS BUILT THE BOTANIC CLINIC AS A PRIVATE MEDICAL FACILITY.

6

1

2

3

1. TOBACCO FIELDS AT PETER'S HOPE.
2. RAINBOW OVER BARROUALLIE.
3. A YOUNG GIRL GRACEFULLY BALANCES SOME GREEN ONIONS THAT SHE HAS REAPED.
4. WOOD CARVER JOSEPH VINCENT DISPLAYS HIS LOVELY MAHOGANY PARROTS FROM HIS WORKSHOP IN LAYOU.
5. SORREL GROWS IN ABUNDANCE AND IS USED FOR PREPARING A TASTY DRINK

4

5

1

P. MICKLES

1. THE IDYLLIC FALLS OF BALEINE LOCATED FAR UP THE LEEWARD COAST.
2. A YOUNG BOY DISPLAYS HIS ARMADILLO AND BREADFRUIT.
3. PULLING A DUG-OUT FISHING BOAT ASHORE IN RICHMOND REQUIRES A LITTLE HELP FROM ONE'S FRIENDS.
4. A REFRESHING DIP IN THE WALLILABOU FALLS.
5. CUMBERLAND BAY IS A FAVORITE ANCHORAGE FOR CRUISING YACHTSMEN.

2

3

4

5

1

SOUTHERN COAST

The southern coast between Arnos Vale and Prospect is the prime residential region. Off this coast is one of the most successful first-class hotels: Young Island Resort. The story of how Young Island received its name is entertaining. Apparently, in the 18th century, Sir William Young, Governor of St. Vincent returned from leave in England and ran into a Carib chief who admired his white charger (in some accounts, a black stallion). With a spontaneous streak of generosity, he gave the horse to the chief. A short while later, the chief noticed Sir Young sitting on the veranda of Government House which at that time was in Calliaqua. Young was staring at the small island across the bay, the chief said: "You like that island, it shall be yours. I give it to you." Thus, the present day name.

To get to this exclusive resort you must take the Young Island water taxi which makes frequent trips from the Young Island Dock on the mainland. Once on the island you are in the midst of a tropical fairyland. The beach on Young Island is fine white sand as are most of the beaches on the southern end of the island.

Fort Duvernette, adjacent to Young Island, was built around 1800. One hundred and ninety-five feet above sea level, it was erected to defend Calliaqua Bay. There are two batteries, one about forty feet from the top of the rock and a second on the summit. Both contain twenty-four pound guns and an eight inch mortar; the entire armament is complete.

On Friday nights, Young Island Resort ferries guests over to Fort Duvernette for a cocktail party. Rum punches are accompanied by fish cakes and coconut chips. A calypso band welcomes the tourist to the rock. The night scene is made more dramatic by the flaming torches.

The area around Villa, Prospect, and Ratho Mill can boast some of the loveliest homes on the island. There are quite a few hotels in this area: Sunset Shores, the Mariners Inn, the Grandview Beach Hotel, Villa Lodge, and Coconut Beach Hotel at Indian Bay. At Ratho Mill is the C.S.Y. Yacht Club with a new hotel right on Blue Lagoon. There are nineteen balconied rooms and a two-tiered swimming pool.

1. YOUNG ISLAND AT SUNSET.
2. C.S.Y CHARTER BOATS DOCKSIDE AT BLUE LAGOON. FORT DUVERNETTE IS SEEN IN THE BACKGROUND.
3. INDIAN BAY WITH BEQUIA IN THE BACKGROUND.

3

1

2

3

4

KENNETH MITCHNICK

1. WATTLE AND DAUB OLD STYLE
HOME IS GIVING WAY TO CONCRETE
BLOCKS!
2. A GIRL, A BOY, AND A KITE SHARE
A TREE.
3. CHILDREN CRACKING ALMONDS.
4. THE LAND IS LUSH AND FERTILE.
5. BAKING BREAD IN A DRUM OVEN.

5

OVERLEAF: WINDWARD COAST FROM UNION PLANTATION

1

1. THE "GREAT HOUSE" AT ORANGE
HILL ESTATES.
2. SALT POND UP THE WINDWARD
COAST NEAR OWIA IS A FAVORITE
SWIMMING HOLE.
3. THE AQUEDUCT AT ORANGE HILL
WAS BUILT AROUND 1859.

On the windward side of the base of the Soufrière lie Orange Hill Estates. Established in 1905, the property occupies 3,200 acres and is one of the largest single coconut estates in the world. In 1964 the crop totaled 8,500,000 coconuts. Formerly a private company owned plantation. The estates are now the center piece of the country's land reform programs. The copra or dried coconut meat is processed into oil which is used for soap, shampoo, margarine, and suntan lotion. Also growing are bananas, citrus fruits, spices, and other vegetables. Manufactured on the estates under an Orange Hill label are lime juice, lime cordial, lime jelly, orange marmalade, grapefruit juice, and coconut shell buttons.

The majority of the workers live in cottages on the estates. The small community has its own carpenters, masons, and mechanics, and grows much of its own produce. Soon the workers will be independent farmers.

2

P. MICKLES

The estates house is set on a rise overlooking the slopes of the land with its gardens and the sea beyond. The long veranda, stately high-ceilinged rooms, and the heavy mahogany furniture all typify the colonial era.

Of historical interest on the estates is a squat stone building near the copra drying ovens. When the plantation used to grow sugarcane in the old days, the cellar under this building was for rum storage. When flames began to shoot from the crater and a black cloud appeared during the 1902 volcanic eruption, forty people who were working nearby crowded into the cellar. The Scottish managers started out in the cellar but fled for the house. They were later found dead, victims of superheated steam from the cloud and lack of oxygen. Those who took refuge in the cellar were the only survivors. The estates which lie under the volcano suffered from the loss of trees and plants and the death of many animals.

3

1

*T*he Soufrière, 4,000 feet above sea level, dominates the northern end of St. Vincent. The name "Soufrière" is of French origin and most likely derived from the word *soufre* which means sulphur, but perhaps the French verb *souffrir* figures in, as it means to suffer.

The first known eruption occurred in 1718. The next documented eruption on April 30, 1812 was actually heard by a British writer at Siba rocks in Demerara, Guyana. The 1812 eruption lasted three days, destroying property and lives. Earlier eruptions have been dated by radiocarbon methods and archeological evidence suggests an eruption as early as 160 A.D. to 350 A.D. A cache of several hundred carved objects thought to be offerings to the god of the volcano were found in the north.

Subsequent to the 1812 eruption, the Soufrière contained two craters one of which held a little lake 1,200 feet below the crater rim. A narrow ridge separated the two craters and a trail around the craters led from one side of the island to the other. The slopes within and without were covered in vegetation. Ninety years went by without a rumble.

The rumble occurred in February 1902. It quickly escalated, but the inhabitants in the north end of the island disregarded the thunderous noises and many refused to leave their homes. On May 7 nineteen earthshocks were experienced and the people of Wallibou, Morne Ronde, and Richmond Estate finally fled. The eruption was much more violent than the previous one. Much tropical vegetation was destroyed. Showers of stones fell even upon the roofs in Kingstown and villages at the south end of the island. The Leeward coast was bombarded with rocks the size of coconuts.

On the Windward side, the residents of Georgetown and the Carib Country were hit the hardest; the villages of Sandy Bay, Overland, Morne Ronde, Wallibou, Waterloo, Orange Hill, Tourama, Fancy, and Lot Fourteen were destroyed. Two thousand people were killed.

Two notable features of the volcanic eruptions are the "dry rivers." The best known are the Wallibou on the Leeward coast and the Rabacca Dry River on the Windward coast. After eruptions from 1812 and 1902, the channels of these streams were filled and choked with scoriae and gravel underneath which the water disappeared as it neared the coast and became subterranean. Sometimes in the rainy seasons water does come down these channels from the mountains.

In 1971 there was a minor eruption and an island of lava formed in the center of the crater lake. On Good Friday, April 13, 1979, the dormant vol-

W.H. HUNT

2

1. THE RABACCA DRY RIVER.
2. THE CRATER OF SOUFRIÈRE.

cano exploded, blasting ash, steam and stones thousands of feet into the air. There were five eruptions on that day, but it took the residents until the second or third eruption to understand the magnitude of what was happening. Only two days before, a check of the volcano indicated that there was no unusual activity. With ash drifting over everything, people in the vicinity of the Soufrière evacuated their homes. Between April 13 and 25, there were twenty explosive eruptions. Earth tremors were recorded on seismographs set up at various points around the volcano, but no serious earthquakes were experienced. There were upward spirals of thick black clouds of ash and cinder suspended in very hot gases rising high over the rim of the crater and cascading down the mountainside. Vulcanologists refer to the clouds as "glowing avalanches when the rock fragments are iridescent."

Luckily, no one was killed in the 1979 explosion, but damage to homes and crops took their toll on the island. Roads had to be repaired, 60% of the banana production was lost, an estimated 285 acres of arrowroot were rendered useless and forest in Larikai, Roseau, and Trois Loup areas were devastated. Many Vincentians were harbored in Bequia until things quieted down. It took time for the ash to settle and for the air to clear.

Today it is once again safe to climb to the Soufrière. To get to the volcano, you can go to Chateaubelair or Richmond on the Leeward side and ask directions on your way or find a guide, or you can ascend from above Georgetown on the Windward side. It is a beautiful hike through a rain forest until the last stretch which is barren and gravelly. It might be chilly at the top and is often quite hazy these days. It is a good idea to bring a picnic lunch. If you take a jeep to the bottom of the trail on the Windward side, the walk up and down will take under six hours.

1979 VOLCANIC ERUPTION

RICHARD FISKE

Soufrière (79)

The thing split Good Friday in two
and that good new morning groaned
and snapped
like breaking an old habit.

Within minutes
people
who had always been leaving nowhere
began arriving nowhere
entire lives stuffed in pillow-cases
and used plastic bags
naked children suddenly transformed
into citizens

'Ologists with their guilty little instruments
were already oozing about the mountainsides
bravely
and by radio

(As a prelude to resurrection and brotherly love
you can't beat ructions and eruptions)

Flies ran away from the scene of the crime
and crouched like Pilate
in the secret places of my house
washing their hands

Thirty grains of sulphur
panicked off the phone
when it rang

Mysterious people ordered
other mysterious people
to go to mysterious places
"immediately"

I wondered about the old woman
who had walked back to hell
to wash her Sunday clothes

All the grey-long day
music
credible and incredibly beautiful
came over the radio
while the mountain refreshed itself

Someone who lives
inside a microphone
kept things in order

Three children
in unspectacular rags
a single bowl of grey dust between them
tried to manure the future
round a young plum tree

The island put a white mask
over its face
coughed cool as history
and fell in love with itself

A bus travelling heavy
cramped as Calvary
thrust its panic into the side of a hovel
and then the evening's blanket
sent like some strange gift from abroad
was rent by lightning.

After a dream
of rancid hope and Guyana rice
I awoke to hear
that the nation had given itself
two hundred thousand dollars

The leaves did not glisten when wet

An old friend
phoned from Ireland
to ask about the future
my Empire cigarettes
have lately been tasting of sulphur

I told her that

SHAKE KEANE

1

TROMSON MONROE

MUSIC

> 1. CONCENTRATING ON THE BEAT.
> 2. A CARNIVAL BEAUTY DISPLAYS HER FEATHERS.
> 3. CARNIVAL COSTUMES TELL A STORY.

Music has always been an integral part of Vincentian culture. Calypso and steel band are the major sounds, although today jazz, classical, electric soulrock, reggae, and even country music can be heard.

A few individuals have been a strong influence on St. Vincent's music scene. Pat Prescod is St. Vincent's foremost serious musician. He is renowned as a brilliant arranger, conductor, pianist and teacher. He has done much to develop music in St. Vincent, most notably with the Kingstown Chorale. Young musicians are also encouraged by the St. Vincent Music Festival held every two years. On the jazz front is St. Vincent's outstanding performer Shake Keane. At one time a commentator for the BBC in England, Shake has played flugle horn and trumpet with bands in England, Germany, and the United States.

Frankie McIntosh, currently a resident in the United States, has arranged and recorded with Calypsonians The Mighty Sparrow and St. Vincent's own Becket, (aka Alston Cyrus) who has had great success with his l.p. "Raw Calypso" and his "Calypso Disco" was featured in the movie "The Deep." Other Becket hits are "Wine Down Kingstown," "Horn Fuh Dem," and "Love is the Answer."

Both Becket and Frankie McIntosh return frequently to be part of St. Vincent's Carnival. Their contributions add enthusiasm and spirit to Carnival participants and spectators.

The country now plans a beautiful Center for the Performing Arts to be designed by Arthur Erickson.

Carnival in St. Vincent dates back before 1920 when it was held at the Botanical Gardens. Carnival started out being a display of folk dances, maypole, stick fights, bois bois and calypso. In the late fifties and early sixties, Carnival was expanded into a beautiful pageant featuring historical bands portraying Roman Emperors, Incas, Greeks, Spaniards, Chinese and North American Indians. Costumes became more and more elaborate. The growth of Carnival over the years and its importance resulted in a change of the date to late June/July, so as not to conflict with the carnival in Trinidad. Besides the visual and auditory sensations, Carnival is also a time of social commentary, political statements, and philosophical expressionism. It's a time of competition, team work, and camaraderie. But most of all, it's a time for fun; time to "Wine down Kingstown!"

3

2

BERTIE DAVIS

BERTIE DAVIS

P. MICKLES

1

1. CARNIVAL COSTUMES ARE ALWAYS
ELABORATE.
2. THE PARADE PASSES BY THE
CATHOLIC CHURCH.

P. MICKLES

2

FISHING

3

*F*ishing is very important to the lives and livelihood of the people in St. Vincent and the Grenadines. There are many methods of fishing: hand-line, trolling, torchlight, trawling, rod or bamboo casting, seining, spearfishing, sprat netting, and the hauling of fishpots. On dark nights, bait-fish, commonly known as ballyhoo, are caught by attracting the fish to the surface with a flambeau.

Seining is a technique wherein fishermen cast their nets encircling a school of fish. Trawling is done by dragging a net on the sea floor as the trawler passes along. Trolling on the other hand is the method of baiting long lines and letting them trail behind a dug-out type sailing canoe, or a moderate speed motorized vessel. The wake of the boat hopefully arouses the attention of some of the larger fish. Hand-line, rod, or bamboo fishing are similar. A fishpot is a wire net or bamboo cage designed so that fish can enter but cannot swim out. Diving for fish with spearguns takes some skill, and although one used to be able to find fish and langouste (island lobster) in shallow enough waters for mask and snorkel, (lobster season is from the beginning of October until the end of April) diving to much deeper depths is now necessary. The most prevalent deep-sea fish are dolphin, bonito, kingfish, mackerel, and red snapper. There are also a host of other species that have local names attached to them. The local fishing boats often bring their larger fish to the hotels first, thus tourists are always sure of finding fresh fish on the menu.

1. FISHING BOATS ON THE BEACH.
2. FISHERMEN BRING THEIR CATCH TO YOUNG ISLAND RESORT. THE HOTEL'S "COCONUT BAR" SITS AFLOAT IN THE BACKGROUND.
3. A YOUNG RASTA IS SELLING REDFISH.

St. Vincent is often called "Gateway to the Grenadines" by cruising sailors. Yachts come from all over the world to sail in the Grenadine waters, which are among the most beautiful. Yearly, the famed 353 foot *Sea Cloud*, formerly owned by Marjorie Merriwether Post cruises the islands. Sleek twelve-meters, traditional gaff-rigged schooners, modern racing boats and huge motor yachts with cars and helicopters on their decks all parade by the Grenadines. There are also charter companies which offer both crewed and bareboat charters. Caribbean Sailing Yachts (C.S.Y.) opened a marina/hotel designed for bareboat charters in Blue Lagoon in 1976. All of their charters in the Windward Islands originate there. Other charter companies such as Stevens Yachts and The Moorings in St. Lucia and Spice Island Charters in Grenada all consider the Grenadines supreme.

For the yachting enthusiast there are both blue water sailing and easy island hops. Coming down the lee of St. Vincent from St. Lucia, you can stop at magnificent Cumberland Bay or at Wallilabou. The more frequented anchorages in St. Vincent are Kingstown Harbor, where you can stock up on fresh food from the market, packaged goods and ice. Then you can carry on a little farther to Young Island or Blue Lagoon; both scenic anchorages.

Crossing the channel to Bequia, you come to Admiralty Bay. Many yachtsmen familiar with Bequia or Bequia's reputation for being so hospitable, make this harbor their landfall from across the Atlantic or from up north.

Bequia has a slipway which can haul yachts and small cargo boats. Water and fuel are also available at the Bequia slip.

Many cruising sailors end up staying in Bequia for months, doing repairs in the Bequia Boatyard or having their sails mended by Simmons Sail Loft, or just because they like it. There are anchorages off Tony Gibbons Beach and around the southside at Friendship Bay and, depending on the weather, at Petit Nevis.

Mustique's Brittania Bay is a favorite among yachtsmen who love to snorkel in the clear waters and to enjoy the soft life at Basil's Bar.

Canouan, Mayreau, Prune Island and Petit St. Vincent all have lovely harbors. The Tobago Cays is a veritable paradise of deserted beaches. There are

1

JILL BOBROW

2

lots of small uninhabited islands where a yachtsman may find himself all alone, such as Isle à Quatre, and Savan. Or, then again, there is the bustling Clifton Harbor at Union Island, where yachtsmen can mingle with fishermen and the island cargo trade.

The prevailing winds are always northeast to south east at 10 to 25 knots. The weather is generally sunny and fair, and the visibility is great. Occasionally, there is low visibility when the phenomenon known as the Sahara Dust kicks up from across the Atlantic, and then the skies are less than perfect. But there is no such thing as fog! There are many cruising guides and charts which clearly identify all the anchorages. Sailing is truly an ideal way to visit the Grenadines.

1. TWO YACHTS RACING DURING BEQUIA EASTER REGATTA.
2. SAILING TOWARDS WESTERN CAY.

THE GRENADINES

The Grenadines are a chain of islands, rocks and islets running for some fifty miles between St. Vincent to the north and Grenada to the south. The political dividing line between the two countries as conceived by the colonial powers, passes through the crystal waters between Petit St. Vincent and Petit Martinique.

With twenty miles of white sand beaches dispersed among coves, inlets, and atolls, the Grenadines are a veritable paradise. All of the islands have something unique to offer in terms of topography and ambience. Besides the lush vegetation, and the sheer beauty of the lands, there are the people, who are very special. They have learned to survive in isolation over the centuries, making a living primarily from the sea. Long dry seasons and a short growing season have had their cultural influence. For instance, every home has its own water system to collect the rain. Small home gardens also thrive among these independent people.

The heritage of the Grenadines is a rich blend from Africa, England, Scotland, France, and New England. The names of the islands superimposed on Carib terminology tell the histories: Bequia, Battowia, Balliceaux, Pillories, Mustique, Petit Mustique, Isle à Quatre, Petit Nevis, Ramay, Savan, Petit Canouan, Canouan, Baleine, Tobago Cays, Mayreau, Catholic, Union, Prune, Petit St. Vincent, and then the rocks and shoals like the Bullet, Sail Rock, and Worlds End Reef. With Mopion and Pinese, it is difficult to know where the sea ends and the island begins.

Yachts cruising from around the world; from Europe to the United States and from the Mediterranean to the Pacific, all make landfall in the Grenadines. Admiralty Bay in Bequia is a particular favorite. The seafaring tradition of the Grenadines means that sailors from the islands have also traveled all over the world on merchant ships and yachts. This experience has given the people of the Grenadines much in common with their yachting visitors.

1

2

GRAYDON MCCREA

1. A FLAMBOYANT TREE IS
SILHOUETTED AGAINST A SUNSET,
ADMIRALTY BAY, BEQUIA.
2. A BOAT IS NEARLY COMPLETED AT
PAGET FARM, BEQUIA.

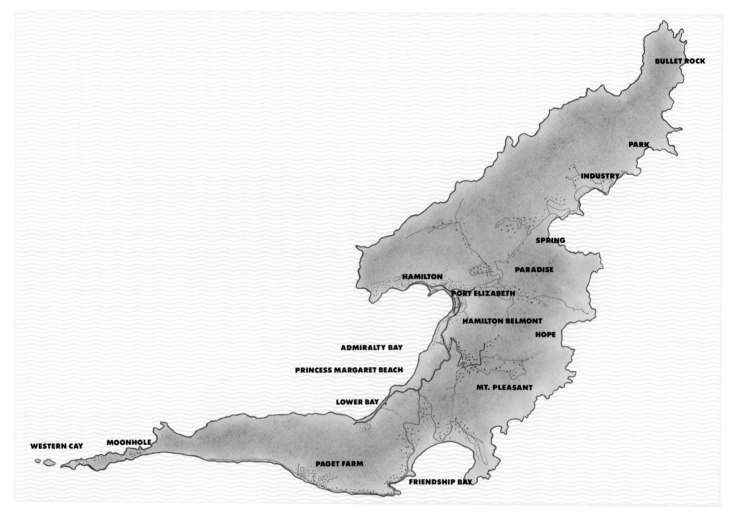

BEQUIA

The name Bequia (pronounced "bekway") comes from an old Carib word "Becouya" meaning Island of the Clouds. The first inhabitants of Bequia were the Arawaks, then the Carib Indians. The more recent history can be traced back through Scottish, English, Irish, French and African ancestry. For instance, over and over again you run into the names Wallace, McIntosh, Ollivierre, Simmons and Quashie. Bequia is nine miles south of St. Vincent and is by far the most developed of the Grenadine Islands. Only nine square miles and with a population of 6,000 this tiny speck on the world is truly a microcosm. Since it is only accessible by boat, hoards of tourists have not yet inundated this small paradise. But it is well known among cruising sailors who often make it their first landfall when crossing the Atlantic. To witness the variety of flags flying off the transoms of the yachts, Admiralty Bay is an international anchorage.

A low-key place, with a handful of restaurants and hotels, Bequia seems to attract repeat visitors. There are two towns or villages: Port Elizabeth which was so named in 1937 in honor of the then Princess Elizabeth is the administrative center on Admiralty Bay, and Paget Farm is a fishing village on the south side of the island. The spirit of the Bequia people is so congenial that visitors enjoy both building and renting houses in their favorite areas whether it be Spring, Hope, Industry, Belmont, Friendship, or some other quiet corner.

When people in Bequia say they are going to town, they invariably mean they are going to Kingstown, St. Vincent. The *Friendship Rose* is a Bequia-built cargo schooner which departs from the town dock in Port Elizabeth every Monday through Friday at 6:30 a.m. and returns from St. Vincent at 12:30. The trip across the channel usually takes about an hour and a half. The motor vessel *Edwina* also makes the daily trip between the two islands.

There are five hotels and a handful of guest houses such as Julie's and Keegan's on the island. Friendship Bay Hotel located on twelve tropical acres overlooking Friendship Bay is the largest with 27 renovated rooms, and under

1

1. THE *FRIENDSHIP ROSE* CROSSING THE BEQUIA CHANNEL.
2. AN AERIAL VIEW OF BEQUIA; AN ISLAND FIRST DESCRIBED BY DUTCH MARINERS.

2

1

new management as of 1984. With a mile of white sandy beach, the hotel looks out over the Grenadines to the south. Also on Friendship Bay is the newly built German-owned Bequia Beach Hotel. Sunny Caribbee's accommodations consist of seventeen cabanas and eight rooms in the colonial-style main house. Located on Admiralty Bay, the atmosphere is serene and peaceful and at the same time offers a full array of watersports and activities from tennis to scuba diving. The Frangipani Hotel, also on Admiralty Bay, owned by Pat and Son Mitchell, and managed by friend Marie Kingston is just a few minutes walk from town. Centrally located for passersby and with a convenient dinghy dock for yachtsmen, the Frangi, as it is affectionately called, is the true meeting place for visitors to Bequia. It has a charming casual ambience and their famous Thursday night barbecue is always well attended. Spring Hotel is the most remote, with only eleven rooms situated on the side of a hill on the grounds of a 200-year-old plantation and overlooking the windward beach of Spring. Here you can play tennis among the palms and the cows. There is a large swimming pool adjacent to the old sugar mill. Bananas and coconuts abound. It's a place where you can truly get away from it all. All of the hotels welcome day visitors to partake of their dining rooms and other facilities upon request.

There are several restaurants on Bequia which are all notable in their own right: Mac's Pizzeria is perhaps the most famous for its consistently delicious treats, and the Harpoon Saloon for sunset cocktails and fresh lobster from their own saltwater pools, and a host of local establishments such as Daphnes, the Green Boley, De Reef, the Old Fig Tree, the Kingfisher Cafe, and the Whaleboner that serve island specialities like pelau, souse, roti and conch.

Bequia is one of those rare places that if you meet anyone from around the world who has spent time there you feel an instant bond with that person.

2

1. CARGO VESSELS ANCHORED IN PORT ELIZABETH.
2. GAMBINI (ON THE LEFT) SELLS HIS HOT SAUCE DAILY UNDER THE ALMOND TREE.
3. TYPICAL GINGERBREAD HOUSE IN BEQUIA.
4. BROKIE IS A WELL KNOWN FACE IN THE HARBOR.

3

4

Axiom

Axiom: you are a sea.
Your eye-
lids curve over chaos

My hands
where they touch you, create
small inhabited islands

Soon you will be
all earth: a known
land, a country.

Margaret Atwood

MARGARET ATWOOD

ADMIRALTY BAY.

71

1

1. AT CHRISTMASTIME ADMIRALTY
BAY IS A VERY BUSY PLACE.
2. AERIAL VIEW OF BEQUIA'S
MAGNIFICENT HARBOR.
3. TONY GIBBONS BEACH.
4. A YOUNG GIRL ENJOYS THE BEACH.
5. WINDSURFING IS RAPIDLY
BECOMING THE NUMBER 1 PASTTIME
IN THE CARIBBEAN WATERS.

2

3

4

5

LOUISE MITCHELL

1

BOATBUILDING

1. MUSICIAN BOB DYLAN'S BOAT WAS
BUILT ON THE BEACH IN BEQUIA.
2. SHIPWRIGHTS AT WORK.
3. LORAN DEWAR IS PUTTING IN THE
KEYPLANK OF A TWENTY FOOT
DOUBLE ENDER.

The people of Bequia are naturally oriented toward the sea; sailing, fishing, boat building, and whaling prevail. Bequians have traveled all over the world on merchant ships and yachts.
Bequians as islanders are dependent on trading, so that the art of boat building has become a natural industry. Functional simplicity and skilled craftsmanship are the key to Bequia boat building. Boats that have been built in Bequia range from double ended sailing dinghies and fishing boats to cargo vessels and sailing yachts. The largest boat ever to have been built in the Caribbean was the *Gloria Colita* a 131-foot schooner, owned and skippered by Reginald Mitchell. The Frangipani Hotel, which has been in the Mitchell family since the turn of the century, was once just the family residence, and the downstairs was a huge storage room which housed the gear from the schooner. The boat traded from Venezuela to the United States but in 1940 she disappeared and was found drifting without a soul aboard in the Bermuda Triangle. More recently, the 68-foot vessel *Water Pearl* was built for the musician Bob Dylan by Californian Chris Bowman and a team of Bequia Shipwrights led by Nolly Simmons and Albert N. Crosby. Another well-known boat built in Bequia was *Plumbelly*, a 25-foot sailboat built by Loren Dewar and German Klaus Alverman who later sailed it single-handed around the world. Loren Dewar still keeps busy building Bequia dinghies at the boatyard. The shipwrights of Bequia have built hundreds of wooden vessels over the years.

2

3

Depending on the size of the boat, and for whom the boat is being built, there is often a big party with goat stew and plenty of rum and music. When a boat is launched in Bequia, many islanders and visitors join in the event.

There is a shop that builds model boats in Hamilton. The Sargeant family takes custom orders for both individualized yachts and production charter boats. Favorite models are the Friendship Rose and the Bequia whaling boats. Even the children of Bequia are involved in boat building, although their proud vessels are made out of coconut shells. The children also race their coconut boats.

GRAYDON MCCREA

3

4

1. FABRICATING MODEL BOATS AT THE
WORKSHOP IN HAMILTON
2. FRESHLY PAINTED MODEL BOATS
HANGING IN THE TREES TO DRY
3. A BOAT IS HAULED AT BEQUIA SLIP
4. EVERYONE HELPS TO LAUNCH A
BOAT
5. A YOUNG BOY SAILS HIS MODEL
BOAT DURING A BEQUIA EASTER
REGATTA

5

1

French Colonial
For Son Mitchell

This was a plantation once,
owned by a Frenchman. The well survives,
filled now with algae, heartcoloured
dragonflies, thin simmer of mosquitoes.

Here is an archway, grown over
with the gross roots of trees,
here's a barred window,
a barn or prison.
Fungus blackens the walls
as if they're burned, but no need:
thickening vines lick over
and through them, a slow
green fire. Sugar,
it was then. Now there are rows
of yellowing limes, the burrows
of night crabs. Five hundred yards
away, seared women in flowered dresses
heap plates at the buffet.
We'll soon join them.
The names of the bays:
Hope, Friendship and Industry.
The well is a stone hole
opening out of darkness,
drowned history. Who knows
what's down there? How many
spent lives, killed muscles.
It's the threshold of an unbuilt
house. We sit on the rim
in the sun, talking
of politics. You could still
drink the water.

MARGARET ATWOOD

KENNETH MITCHNICK

2

3

4

1. VIEW FROM MT. PLEASANT
2. THE WINDWARD COAST OF BEQUIA;
INDUSTRY BAY AND PARK
3. TENNIS COURTS AT SPRING
4. THE OLD SUGAR MILL AT SPRING
PLANTATION

PAT MITCHELL

1

2

One area that has achieved a certain amount of fame from *National Geographic* is Moonhole. West of Paget Farm, there is a private development of seventeen houses designed by American Tom Johnston. The houses are imaginatively built of stone, hanging off cliffs, or sometimes swallowed up by them. George Stark of the Washington Redskins keeps a home here. This unusual community derives its name from an arched rock formation on the water's edge. Villagers at Paget Farm say the space seen through the empty rock circle captures the sky in such a way that it looks like a moon peaking through. Moonhole, the rock and the houses continue to be a curiosity.

4

1. LOOKING OUT OVER FIELDS OF
PIGEON PEAS AT FRIENDSHIP BAY.
2. THE JENNINGS HOUSE AT
MOONHOLE WITH AN ARCH TO
NOWHERE.
3. A WHALEBONE BAR.
4. THE ORIGINAL "MOONHOLE,"

3

Cassava farine is a crumbly starchy food which once processed keeps indefinitely. It needs no further cooking and can be used in a variety of ways but most often in broths and fish dishes. The root is grated and squeezed by wringing in a cloth to eliminate highly toxic hydrocyanic acid. It is then baked by stirring over a fire in a large metal "copper," a cast iron utensil originally brought from England for the sugar industry.

1

LINDA RASMUUSEN

1. BAKING THE CASSAVA.
2. A WOMAN IS SIFTING THE CASSAVA THROUGH A SEA FAN.
3. FISHING BOATS IN PAGET FARM ARE ALWAYS BRIGHTLY PAINTED.

2

LINDA RASMUUSEN

3

The Bequia Easter Regatta is an annual event that was started in 1967. The race includes events for all classes of boats, yachts, workboats, and fishing boats. The racing course varies for the different classes of boats. One race begins in the harbor with a push off start from the beach, out to Western Cay, around a mark at Paget Farm and back again. Other courses involve marks at Isle à Quatre, and Petit Nevis. There is also a single handed circumnavigation of Bequia. On shore, in the past few years at a local establishment called De Reef, festivities, food, and dancing prevail. Prizes are awarded and tourists, locals, and regulars join together in the spirit of competitive fun.

1. PLOTTING TACTICS FOR THE RACE.
2. WING ON WING.
3. THE START ON THE BEACH.
4. THE SAILING DINGHY WENDY SKIPPERED BY ALEC.

1

2

ELIZABETH FLANNIGAN

3

ELIZABETH FLANNIGAN

1

WHALING

The Grenadines have been the hunting grounds of whalers since the late nineteenth century. American whalers from places like New Bedford, Massachusetts came to the Grenadines in search of sperm whales, humpbacks, and pilot whales (also known as blackfish). Humpback whales in particular are frequent visitors to tropical waters.

The Yankee whalers took on local apprentices. One of the Bequia men employed in 1860 was William Thomas Wallace. He traveled to New Bedford, learned the whaling trade, then returned to Bequia with his American bride, Estella Francis Curren. During the 1870s Wallace started the first whaling company in the Grenadines. He was not very successful because at that time there was a lot of competition from Norweigan whalers who slaughtered most of the sought-after humpbacks.

Wallace shut down his whaling enterprise and went to Scotland where he learned the share basis system of whaling. He returned to Bequia in the 1880s, and the whaling industry became well-established with its base at Friendship Bay. Wallace joined forces with Frenchman Joseph Ollivierre who owned Paget Farm Estate and maintained a separate whaling station at a small island offshore called Petit Nevis.

In 1890 six whaling fisheries were operating in Bequia, one at Canouan, and one at Frigate Rock. Whalers would go out in twenty-six foot open doubled-ended boats and when a whale was caught, the meat, bones, and teeth were distributed to the crews and sold to the islanders. The owners of the boats would maintain the boats, repair and paint them, and supply all the necessary equipment. This meant that one third of the share went to the owners, one third to the officers, and one third was divided equally among the crews of the companies.

In the 1920s and 1930s humpbacks became very scarce as a result of indiscriminate killing of mothers and calves. Whaling cooperatives declined although there is still some whaling going on in Bequia today.

PAT MITCHELL

1. THE LAUNCHING OF WHY ASK, THE LATEST WHALEBOAT BUILT IN BEQUIA.
2. ATHNEAL OLLIVIERRE; THE CHIEF HARPOONER.
3. EPHRAIM BYNOE (L.) AND FERDIE ADAMS (R) ARE LOOKING OUT FOR WHALES.
4. PETIT NEVIS. THE WHALING STATION.
5. HARPOONING A WHALE.

DAVID EMANUEL

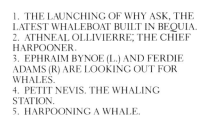

LINDA RASMUUSEN

LEE AUSTIN

GRAYDON MCCREA

1

Every year from February to May after their boats have been blessed by the Anglican priest, the Bequia whalers go out to hunt whales. As soon as the topic of whaling is mentioned, someone bemoans the fate of the poor whales, but whaling done as a million dollar industry by the Russians and Japanese has nothing in common with Bequia whaling. Bequia whalers with their open boats and harpoons are employing the same methods that Nantucket whalers used two centuries ago.

The whale boats are twenty-six feet long with ribs and decking made of local white cedar. The exterior planking is hand-hewn from imported white pine. Under sail, the boats can reach fifteen knots surfing. They are launched into Friendship Bay with large rocks providing the ballast. There are five oars per boat, in addition to the sails, mainsail, and jib. No engines can be used as this would alert the whales.

With a lookout perched on Monkey Hill in Bequia, the two boats head for Mustique where they have a good panoramic view. Here the twelve men sit peering at the seascape searching for the telltale spout or breech. With a cry of "Blows, man, blows!" they hurtle down the hill to launch the two boats in pursuit. Both boats narrow in for the kill.

Athneal Ollivierre is the most skilled harpooner. If he makes a lucky thrust, he hits the whale and the tether connected to the harpoon unravels and is made fast to the boat. A second harpoon is then thrown at the whale. The whale takes the small boat for what is known as the Nantucket sleigh ride. Sometimes, the whale must be lanced several times before it acquiesces.

As part of the final kill, the harpooner jumps on the whale's back and jabs in one last time. Then quickly, the whale's mouth is sewn up so that it will not take on water and sink while it is being towed to Petit Nevis where it will be butchered. Lincoln Simmons, Bequia's famous sailmaker, has been the butcher for the last several decades.

Since years go by and no whales are caught, and other years only one or two

1. LOOKING OUT FOR WHALE SPOUTS.
2. LOUIS OLLIVIERRE LOOKS ON AS THE MEAT IS BEING CUT UP.
3. DANIEL HAZEL IS THE HELMSMAN OF THE WHALEBOAT.
4. LINCOLN-SIMMONS IS BUTCHERING THE WHALE.

PAT MITCHELL

are captured, whaling often seems to be more of a ritual in Bequia than an ongoing economic consideration. Still, the people of Bequia, long accustomed to whale meat, eagerly await a catch. Almost the whole island gathers on the offshore whale cay to claim their piece of whale. Some of the women salt down strips right there and even cook or dove huge pots of it in its own oil, after which it will keep indefinitely. In the days before refrigeration (a luxury even now) this was of prime importance to a people living an isolated existence. Now many of the twelve whalermen are in their 60s and 70s and the harpooner Athneal Ollivierre is 64 years old. None of the younger men seem interested in this dangerous and financially unrewarding life work so that in all likelihood, these skills will soon pass out of existence. It is partly this that has encouraged some interested Bequia persons to start a local museum, the Bequia Whaling & Sailing Museum, due to open in 1986.

ADMIRALTY BAY AT SUNSET.

FIREWORKS ON NEW YEARS EVE.

MUSTIQUE

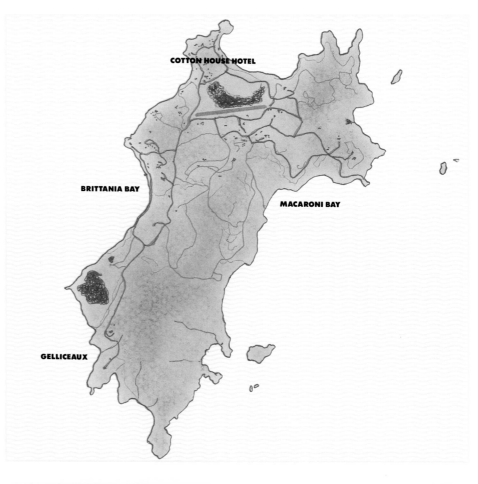

COTTON HOUSE HOTEL

BRITTANIA BAY

MACARONI BAY

GELLICEAUX

1

2

When do you hear the names Princess Margaret and Mick Jagger spoken in the same breath? It is probably only in relation to the island of Mustique. Mustique is an island eighteen miles south of St. Vincent. It is approximately 1½ by 3 miles, covering 1,400 acres. Surrounded by coral reefs, coves, and sandy beaches, the interior is hilly with a large plain to the north. Mount St. George is the highest elevation at 495 feet above sea level. The name "Mustique" comes from the French meaning mosquito. That is hardly the image this island projects now. Mustique has been developed into one of the most exclusive communities in the world.

Mustique's history is similar to the rest of the Grenadines. The Arawaks, then the Caribs, are known to have lived there, and artifacts such as burial pots dating from the seventh and eighth centuries have been discovered. In 1835 the Hazell family acquired the island and grew sugar and cotton, until the abolition of slavery precipitated the decline of the sugar market.

A wealthy Scottish nobleman, the Honorable Colin Tennant, purchased Mustique from the Hazells in 1958. He had a vision of developing the island into the ultimate hideaway for the "rich and the famous." He has since sold to the Venezuelans but still chairs the company.

There is one hotel, The Cotton House, and one small guest house on the island. The hotel is a nineteen room West Indian Inn built around an eighteenth century cotton warehouse and sugar mill. The hotel is owned by Guy de la Houssaye, who also owns the Bakoua Beach Hotel in Martinique. The Cotton House was renovated and redesigned by the late Oliver Messel. Built of rock and coral, distinctive features are the cedar shutters and arched louvered doors. The timbered main lounge is a spacious two stories high and appointed with antiques, hammered leather screens, Spanish mirrors, ivory, and silver collectibles. The Cotton House is a blend of tropical simplicity accented with kitsch oddities like the shell fountain and the opulent cabinet amply impregnated with shells. You really get a feeling what plantation life must have been like around tea time when you sit on the wide veranda and let your thoughts wander. Accommodations are bouganvillea covered bungalows off the main house and around the pool. The swimming pool with its Romanesque ruins is a good example of Messel's whimsical imagination.

There are currently fifty-two houses on Mustique. All are privately owned but most of them are available for rent. The design of the houses and their situations vary from Moorish castles on hilltops to classical northern European on beachfronts. Building sites are available for additional residences. The granite and basaltic stones used in construction are quarried on the

1. BRITTANIA BAY OFFERS A PROTECTED YACHT ANCHORAGE AND THE ADDED ATTRACTION OF BASIL'S BAR.
2. MACARONI BEACH.

1. THE OLD SUGAR MILL HAS BEEN
CONVERTED INTO A BOUTIQUE.
2. THE COTTON HOUSE USED TO BE
AN EIGHTEENTH-CENTURY COTTON
WAREHOUSE UNTIL IT WAS
RENOVATED BY THE LATE OLIVER
MESSEL.

island. These blended with South American hardwoods are a regular theme in Mustique architecture. Rainfall is limited, therefore, houses must be built with efficient rain cachements. There are several creative architects who are involved with the Mustique houses. People who come to Mustique seek privacy and service. The clientele is an even mix of North and South Americans, British and Europeans.

There is an airfield which is being extended to 3,000 feet and widened to 60 feet. It is suitable for light aircraft of the Islander, Aero-Commander, or Beechcraft Baron type. Commercial and charter flights available from St. Vincent and Barbados. The bamboo airport building is quite charming.

The islanders who live and work on Mustique number about 250 and there are another 350 transient construction workers mainly from St. Vincent.

One of the main tourist attractions besides the nine deserted white sandy beaches is the notorious wreck of the *Antilles*. The 20,000 ton French ocean liner, in an apparent attempt to get a closer peek at Mustique, ran aground on a coral reef off the northern coast of the island. The passengers were rescued by the QE2, but the boat was a total loss. As it deteriorated from day to day, much of its contents were either salvaged or scavenged. The still visible rusting hull is the subject of many anecdotes.

Besides the usual recreational activities of watersports and tennis, horseback riding is also offered, but the real hot spot on the island is Basil's Bar. Originally a ramshackle hut on the jetty, the bar has developed into an alfresco restaurant and occasional disco. The party-of-the-week is the Wednesday night barbecue, where a sumptuous buffet of fresh fish or perhaps roast suckling pig is accompanied by a host of side dishes. The music is calypso, soul, rock, or reggae. Here the yachtsmen mingle with the island dwellers. The bar is located on Brittania Bay, the main yacht harbor.

Charter boats and world famous yachts enjoy the clear beautiful waters surrounding Mustique. Perhaps Mustique should be renamed Mystique.

1

2

1

1. THE GINGERBREAD HOUSE WAS ONE OF THE FIRST HOUSES BUILT ON MUSTIQUE.
2. THE HOUSEKEEPER'S DAUGHTER KIZZIANNE ENJOYS THE HAMMOCK.
3. PASTEL PINK WITH CRISP WHITE TRIM, THE HOUSE COMBINES BOTH CHARM AND WHIMSY.
4. THERE IS AN OPEN AIR CUPOLA A FEW STEPS FROM THE LIVING ROOM—THE PERFECT PLACE TO HAVE BREAKFAST AND GAZE AT THE SEA.

2

3

4

The Gingerbread House was one of the first houses built on Mustique. Pastel pink with crisp white trim, the house combines both charm and whimsy. There is an open air cupola a few steps away from the living room—the perfect place to have breakfast and gaze at the sea. The beach is just a walk away, but the pool affords a comfortable spot to relax and read.

1

1. THE AERIAL VIEW OF MUSTIQUE
SHOWS THE WRECK OF THE ANTILLES.
2. BASIL CHARLES OF BASIL'S BAR
FAME.
3. THE BEACH HOUSE IS A
MULTILEVELED CONSTRUCTION.
4. A PRIVATE STAIRWAY TO A
SECLUDED BEACH.
5. BAMBOO AND RATTAN ARE THE
FASHION HERE.

It was love at first sight! When I stumbled upon the isle of Mustique, some six years ago, I was surprised to find such a garden spot so close to the front lines of the big city. It was as though I'd stepped out of the hurly burly of New York right into paradise and I was amazed that it wasn't over-crowded! Could it be, I wondered, that there were no high-rise hotels, no food chains and no swarms of rabid tourists? I had to keep pinching myself in case the whole thing turned out to be a mirage.

But no, fortunately for me it wasn't. Battle weary from a hectic schedule, I was able to find a place to relax in comfort and above all privacy. Since that day, Mustique has supplied myself and my husband Andre with a home away from home—a retreat from the wicked world of "show biz" and an oasis far from the maddening crowds.

The special ambience and style of Mustique, is no accident, however. It is the brainchild of its founder, Lord Glenconner, a.k.a. Colin Tennant, who had the vision and foresight to enlist the collaboration of the gifted architect Oliver Messel and together they supervised the development of a colony of beautifully designed private homes, the graciousness of which rival anything I've seen, from Beverly Hills to the French Riviera.

Mustique is one of the satellite islands of St. Vincent, the Flagship to all the smaller Grenadine Islands. It is the beauty, gentleness, and hospitality of the people of St. Vincent that make it possible for a place like Mustique to exist. St. Vincent, the agricultural center of the Grenadines, exports food, craftsmanship and services to Mustique and is also a beauty spot itself—well worth a visit.

For the inhabitants of Mustique, it's the pot of gold at the end of the rainbow…where all the hard work pays off. Visiting us there recently from New York, a friend remarked that the island itself seemed like a fantasy world. My husband answered, "No, what you've just come from is a fantasy. This is the *real thing*!" He was right. On Mustique, real life is like a dream come true.

Raquel Welch

Raquel Welch

2

3

THE BEACH HOUSE

4

5

Harding and Mary Lawrence have traveled worldwide and have chosen Mustique as a second home. They are in the process of building a spectacular palazzo atop Mustique's highest hill. In the meantime, they reside in the "Beach House," a multileveled construction built into a cliff overlooking azure water and coral reefs and silky crescent beach. Partly fabricated of bamboo and elegantly furnished with straw rugs and rattan furniture, there is a feeling of freshness and the great outdoors. In fact, clement weather is so predictable that windows and doors remain permanently open. Great long stairs lead down to the beach and to the low level porch. The back drop is a cavelike ledge with cascading water. A bar and lounge chairs and perpetual shade comfort the sun weary.

March 8, 1985

Dear Prime Minister:

We are fortunate to have traveled throughout the world and to have lived in a wide variety of places such as Texas, Arizona, California, New York, Mexico,and France. In our free moments we have duly examined most of the sunny seas and islands from Bali to Barbados. So when we found the Grenadines and fell deeply in love, we knew for certain there is nothing better around the next corner. We knew we had found, at last, the most beautiful, unspoiled, serene islands anywhere. That such paradise is so welcoming to strangers seems to us one of the wonders of this complicated world! Our search is over. We are Home—two of the luckiest people alive—we know without a doubt.

Warm regards,

Mary Lawrence

Mary Lawrence

CANOUAN

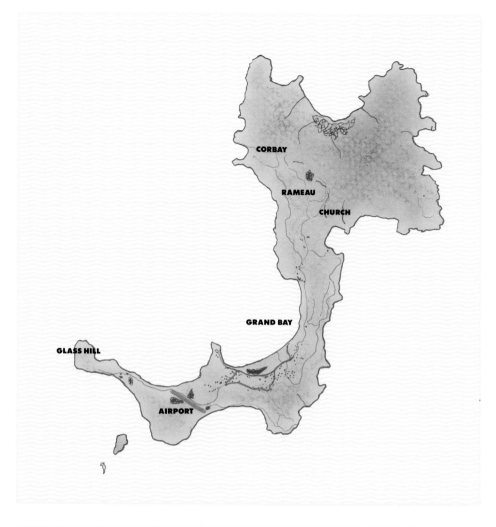

1

T wenty-five miles south of St. Vincent is the small crescent shaped island of Canouan. It is 3½ miles by 1½ miles and its highest peak is 855 feet. It is a quiet island, totally unspoiled by tourism. During the dry season the island is characterized by prominant yellow and brown hills. Sometimes the name of the island is spelled "Cannouan," which recalls the Carib name of Cannoun, meaning Turtle Island. It was here that the ship building industry in the Grenadines started. Then, the owner of the island

2

1. GRAND BAY.
2. SCHOOLCHILDREN EAGER TO HAVE THEIR PICTURES TAKEN.
3. THE REEFS AROUND CANOUAN ARE CLEARLY DEFINED.

3

himself an architect, brought the shipwright Benjamin Compton from Hampshire, England after the abolition of slavery. The deserted old church with its magnificent steeple, secluded in the wilderness on the northern side of the island testifies to a former glory. A hurricane in 1921 swept away the village from around the church. The new village was then built on the other side of the island.

There are numerous anchorages around the island. Corbay and Rameau

1

2

are in idyllic deserted spots, but there is no access ashore (the beaches there are minimal), and there is often quite a swell. Grand Bay is the main anchorage for yachtsmen, but the waters tend to be rolling. The Grenadines has many great beaches but none better than on the eastern side of Canouan protected by an extensive reef. There are two hotels: the French-owned Canouan Beach Hotel, and the Crystal Sands Beach Hotel.

Walking around the island, you get the feeling that you are a true explorer in a primitive land. The people are shy but friendly. They are mostly fishermen and farmers. Hiking overland to private coves is both possible and worthwhile. Even though Canouan is undeveloped, there is an airstrip on the island, so it won't be long before the outside world invades.

3

1. THE ANGLICAN CHURCH.
2. A HERMIT CRAB.
3. THE CRYSTAL WATERS AT CANOUAN
BEACH HOTEL.
4. SESAME IS GROWN IN CANOUAN
AND THE LOCALS CALL IT "BENNA".

4

MAYREAU

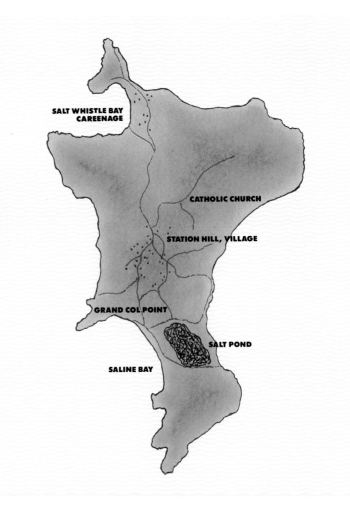

1

Mayreau is a tiny place of 1½ square miles with less than one hundred people, many goats, and a few sheep. The people make their living from the sea: sailors and fishermen. Mayreau is French in history and religion. A French family, the Saint Heliers, were the first settlers. They brought with them Roman Catholicism, which still passionately prevails in this secluded community today. A descendant of the St. Heliers is now Governor General of St. Vincent and the Grenadines.

There are no roads or cars, but there is a charming little church. The local priest is quite receptive to visitors and prepared to spend time chatting about the island and his work. The view from the hilltop church is indeed worthwhile, with a panoramic view of Canouan, Tobago Cays, Petit St. Vincent, Union, and Grenada.

Rimmed by lovely, virgin beaches, Mayreau has two harbors with good anchorages for yachtsmen. Salt Whistle Bay is a name right out of a Herman Wouk novel. On shore nestled into the trees is a new low-key resort with a bar/restaurant and a boutique. One can walk across the lowland to the beach on the windward side where shells and driftwood wash ashore. There is also a trail to the village. Not far away is an abandoned cultivation of aloe vera, and on the flats an original salt pond that produces beautiful crystals of rock salt in the dry season.

Saline Bay's waterfront is lined with sea grapes. Here there is also a path leading to the village and past the salt pond to more beaches on the windward side.

2

1. FISHING BOATS DOT THE
SHORELINE.
2. THE CATHOLIC CHURCH ON
MAYREAU PLAYS AN IMPORTANT ROLE
IN THE LIVES OF THE INHABITANTS.

2

1

2

1. THE BEACH AT SALINE BAY HAS A
PATH TO THE VILLAGE.
2. A TYPICAL HOUSE IN THE VILLAGE.
3. SUNSET VIEW FROM THE TOP OF
THE HILL LOOKING TOWARDS UNION.
4. AERIAL PHOTOGRAPH OF MAYREAU.
5. MAYREAU IS A LOW-KEY PLACE
WITH NO ROADS OR CARS.

3

4

5

OVERLEAF: TOBAGO CAYS

107

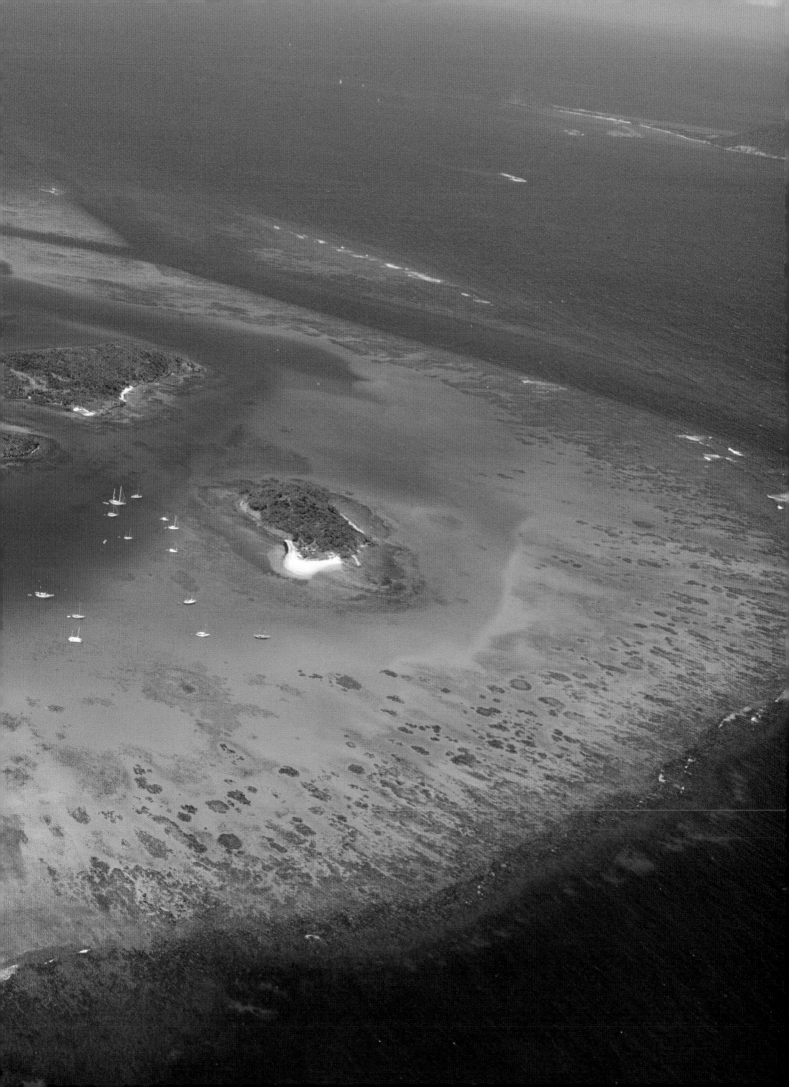

1. FROLICKING IN THE TOBAGO CAYS.
2. FRESH FISH IN TIME FOR LUNCH.
3. SNORKELING IS A FAVORITE PASTTIME IN THESE WATERS.
4. THIS LOCAL BOAT RUNS DAY CHARTERS OUT OF UNION.
5. THE REEFS AROUND THE TOBAGO CAYS ARE TOUTED TO BE AMONG THE BEST IN THE WORLD.

1

2

TROMSON MONROE

3

4

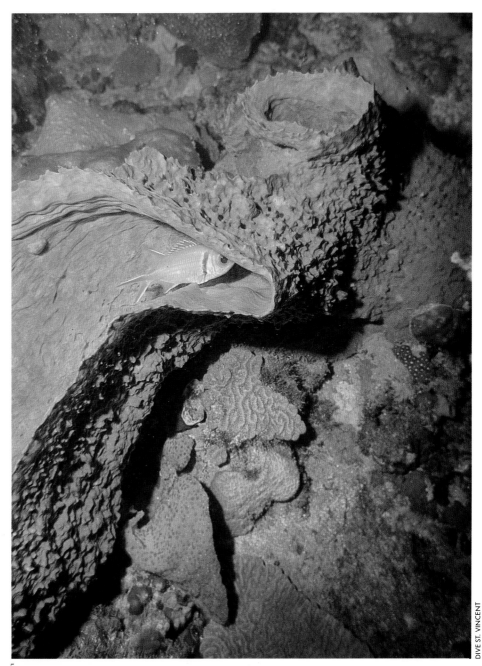

5

DIVE ST. VINCENT

No one sails through the Caribbean without anchoring in the legendary Tobago Cays. The Tobago Cays, not to be confused with the island of Tobago near Trinidad, are a cluster of five uninhabited islets off Mayreau. They are surrounded by coral and sand shoals and are famous for spectacularly clear water and a wealth of multicolored fish. The islands are protected from the sea by a horseshoe reef. Anchoring near the reef allows access to some of the most fabulous snorkeling in the Caribbean and at the same time affords a vista of the great Atlantic. Occasionally fishermen set up campsites on the shores of the Tobago Cays.

In 1983 a whale mysteriously found its way into the Tobago Cays but could not seem to find its way out. Like a scene out of Walt Disney, local charter boats would anchor and wait for the whale to swim by and surface. The whale seemed totally unafraid of people, even curious. Some regular whale watchers would tie their dinghies a short way from their boats, wait for the whale to visit, then quietly slip into the water and swim with it. One catamaran that runs frequent day charters to the Cays from Petit St. Vincent even tried communicating with the whale by placing a tape of Judy Collins whale songs in the pontoons of the vessel. The whale, fortunately, found his way out to the ocean after several months.

PRUNE
(PALM) ISLAND

1

2

On the charts it is still labeled as Prune Island. However, in 1966, Texan Johnny Caldwell secured a ninety nine year lease for ninety nine dollars and created the Palm Island Hotel Company. He planted multitudinous palm trees and developed an imaginative resort. The Palm Island Beach Club offers quiet unpretentious bungalows with wooden slat louvers and sliding glass doors that open onto patios. A stone trail winds its way from cottage to cottage and meanders among the sea grapes and the ubiquitous palms. The random flow of charterboats anchor off Casuarina Beach, but the most unusual sight is the Sun Princess cruise ship of "Love Boat" fame. The windward side of the island is a good bet for beachcombing. Little else is happening, but that's exactly why people fly to Union Island to be ferried to Palm Island—to get away from it all.

3

1. AERIAL OF PRUNE ISLAND.
2. THE CRUISE SHIP DWARFS THE ISLAND.
3. UNION ISLAND IN THE BACKGROUND.
4. JUST A FEW PALM TREES.

4

UNION ISLAND

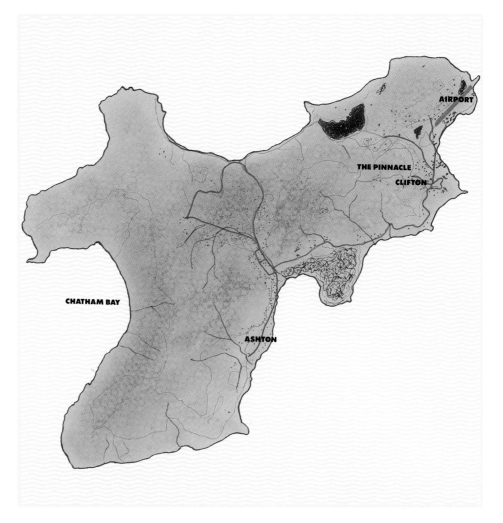

Covering 2,150 acres, the topography of the island is dramatically mountainous. Because of its ridges and peaks profiled on the horizon, Union has been compared to Tahiti. The peaks are loftily named Mt. Parnassus and Mt. Olympus. The island measures three miles by one mile.

Union Island was for the most part a single plantation belonging to the Richards family and divided up among the inhabitants in 1911 into four and six acre plots.

Compared to Mayreau and Canouan, Union is much more developed. There is an airport with scheduled commercial flights that also services Petit St. Vincent and Palm Island. Union is St. Vincent's southern point of entry for customs clearance for yachts. Clifton Harbor, protected by Newlands Reef, and Ashton, another smaller town on Union were probably settled by Bristol sailors because their names reflect towns outside of Bristol in the United Kingdom. Most of the population lives in Ashton which rests beneath Mt. Parnassus. Both the Anchorage Hotel and the Sunny Grenadines offer services for yachtsmen. Clifton has several shops and boutiques offering local handicrafts as well as imported items. Clifton Beach Hotel is owned by Conrad Adams, a Union Islander. So is the Sunny Grenadines run by the retired seaman King Mitchell. The Anchorage Hotel is the most posh establishment on the island and has a distinctly French flavor in language and cuisine. After all with the Union Island airport, built by the Martiniquan André Beaufrand, Paris is accessible in one day via Fort de France.

Hiking on Union bears unpredictable rewards. Although the terrain is rugged, the people are friendly and interesting. Of particular interest is the beautiful Big Sand beach, and the secluded harbor of Chatham Bay.

1

2

1. A WOMAN WATCHES AS FISH ARE BEING SOLD
2. CLIFTON HARBOR IS RAPIDLY BECOMING A FAVORITE YACHTING CENTER
3. ENTERING CLIFTON HARBOR FROM THE SEA

3

1

1. BIG SAND.
2. SELLING A BOATLOAD OF FISH.
3. A LOCAL BOAT BETWEEN THE
PEAKS OF UNION.
4. HANDICRAFT SHOP IN CLIFTON.
5. AERIAL PHOTO OF UNION.

2

3

4

5

1

2

3

4

1. FRIGATE ISLAND OFF THE
SOUTHEAST COAST OF UNION.
2. THE CATHOLIC CHURCH.
3. THERE'S NO DOUBT ABOUT WHICH
WAY TO GO.
4. CARGOBOATS ARE OFFLOADING AT
THE TOWN DOCK.

1

1. LOOKING OUT OVER UNION ISLAND.
2. HAMMOCKS ON THE BEACH.
3. BLUE-BITCH STONE DOMINATES THE
CONSTRUCTION OF THE GUEST
QUARTERS.
4. SUNFISHING AROUND THE ISLAND.
5. THE CLEAR WATERS ENCIRCLING P.S.V.
ARE TRULY EVIDENT IN THIS AERIAL
PHOTOGRAPH.

Afficionados of the Grenadines need not inquire what the initials P.S.V. stand for. For those who don't read the small advertisements in *The New Yorker* and don't travel with a copy of *Relais et Chateaux*, P.S.V. is Petit St. Vincent. Southernmost of the St. Vincent Grenadines, this unique island resort is forty miles south of St. Vincent.

To get to P.S.V. you fly to Union Island where you are met at the airport and ferried to the island in a motor launch. The owner, Hazen Richardson is your cordial host. Haze has been involved in the development of the resort from the beginning. Construction of the island began in 1966 and was completed in December of 1968. There are twenty two cottages all made of native "blue-bitch" stone, quarried from the island itself. The woods used are purple heart and green heart, brought up from Guyana.

Whether on hilltop or shoreside, the cottages are strategically placed to afford the maximum privacy. Patios from every cottage offer spectacular views. Meals are served in the main pavillion which overlooks the harbor. If you prefer, however, you can take all of your repasts in the privacy of your villa. Since there are no telephones in the cottages, there is an alternative communications system. At the entrance to your walkway is a flagpole and a bamboo mailbox. You simply slip a request for poached eggs and champagne into your box and raise the flag.

White silky beaches and utterly translucent water encircle the island. There are two tiny cays nearby. They are called Pinese and Mopion which mean bedbug and louse. Mopion, easily reached by Hobiecat or Sunfish, has a small thatch shelter on it and is the prototype of the deserted island cartoon.

Being an island resort, the sea becomes the major theme of P.S.V. Often the anchorage is replete with magnificent yachts which always adds a little color to the already magnificent scenic back drop.

Most of the resorts in the Grenadines have a special barbecue or "jump up" night. They all seem to rotate nights so that if you are on a charter boat you can attend one everynight of the week. P.S.V. sets up tables on the beach with torches planted in the sand and offers classical piano music by moonlight.

PETIT
ST. VINCENT

2

3

5

4

BRUCE WOLF

1

1. SNORKELING IN THESE WATERS IS
AMONG THE FINEST THE CARIBBEAN
HAS TO OFFER.
2. DID HE REALLY FIND THAT BOTTLE OF
CHAMPAGNE IN THE SEA?
3. AN ARCHED DOORWAY LEADS TO A
LOVELY PATIO OF ONE OF THE
COTTAGES.
4. THIS HILLTOP VILLA OVERLOOKING
THE ATLANTIC OFFERS SWEEPING VIEWS
AND ASSURES TOTAL PRIVACY.

2

JILL BOBROW

JILL BOBROW

3

4

BRUCE WOLF

Sunset II

Sunset, now that we're finally in it
is not what we thought.

Did you expect this violet black
soft edge to outer space, fragile as blown ash
and shuddering like oil, or the reddish
orange that flows into
your lungs and through your fingers?
The waves smooth mouthpink light
over your eyes, fold after fold.
This is the sun you breathe in,
pale blue. Did you
expect it to be this warm?

One more goodbye,
sentimental as they all are.
The far west recedes from us
like a mauve postcard of itself
and dissolves into the sea.

Now there's a moon,
an irony. We walk
north towards no home,
joined at the hand.

I'll love you forever,
I can't stop time.

This is you on my skin somewhere
in the form of sand.

Margaret Atwood
MARGARET ATWOOD

FLORIDA

ATLANTIC OCEAN

BAHAMAS

LEEWARD ISLANDS

WINDWARD ISLANDS

CARIBBEAN SEA

THE CARIBBEAN

ST. VINCENT

BEQUIA

BATTOWIA

ISLE À QUATRE

BALLICEAUX

MUSTIQUE

SAVAN

CANOUAN

TOBAGO CAYS

MAYREAU

PALM ISLAND

UNION ISLAND

PETIT ST. VINCENT